ST JOHN'S
WINCHESTER CHARITY

Detail from *Treatise on the Kalendar, and Surgical Drawings*, *c.*1100, in the Hunter 100 manuscript. These Benedictine monks were famous for their medical and surgical skills. (By permission of the Dean and Chapter of Durham.)

ST JOHN'S
WINCHESTER CHARITY

Barbara Carpenter Turner

Phillimore

1992

Published by
PHILLIMORE & CO. LTD.
Shopwyke Hall, Chichester, Sussex

ISBN 0 85033 843 3

Printed and bound in Great Britain by
BIDDLES LTD.
Guildford, Surrey

'... *and I have redde that S. Brinstane founded an hospitale yn Wynchester.*'

(John Leland *c.*1435)

Contents

List of Illustrations

Frontispiece: Surgical drawing, *c.* 1100

Preface and Acknowledgements

The hospitals of medieval Hampshire were of various kinds. The town hospitals were used by the local poor and sick; they received beggars at the town gates, sometimes reasonably wealthy travellers and pilgrims, and even the occasional crusader. The monastic hospitals were infirmaries caring for the religious of a particular house, and also for the families of the monks and nuns who could not otherwise make provision for their own kin.

Any hospital dedicated to St Mary Magdalen belonged to a particular house dealing with leprosy, recalling the story of Jesus, St Mary Magdalen and her pot of precious ointment. These were places where few patients had any hope of recovery, and men and women had to stay in isolation until they died. The Lepers' House in Winchester was substantial. There were similar isolated houses in Hampshire dedicated the same way; St Mary Magdalene in Southampton was one such, 'Le M Maudeleyne', which seems to have been founded by Southampton citizens as a refuge for lepers and which appears in the town accounts by 1172. The lepers received a pittance of ale from the Southampton Guild.

Some hospitals have very well documented histories, including St Julian's, God's House, in Southampton, with its magnificent tower which still makes a marvellous contribution to that city's landscape. It was formerly a town hospital for the poor, founded and generously endowed by wealthy citizens in the reign of Richard I, which took in men as well as women, but not lepers. From 1343 it belonged to Queen's Hall, a new Oxford foundation. The infirmaries for men and women in St Julian's had been separated, and there was a large establishment including a warden, a priest and domestic staff. The poor inhabitants were occasionally employed in work for the warden and the hospital, and some wardens used the place for the benefit of their poor relations, a common enough feature of medieval life. In 1538 St Julian's had three priests to pray for the souls of the founder and Edward IV, and it housed six poor brothers, four poor sisters, and some beggars 'indigent and infirm'. It spent £28 a year on wayfarers, strangers beyond the seas and the poor at the gate. There was a butler, a cook, an undercook and a washerwoman, and it was a well-administered establishment, in many ways in its care for the poor not unlike a monastery. In its later years it housed the 'French Church' in Southampton – a congregation of Walloon refugees. Its substantial endowment, and the fact that it passed to an Oxford college, probably made it one of the most successful of all the town hospitals in Hampshire. It is useful to compare it briefly with St John's of Winchester, but also to compare the latter house with the other Hampshire hospitals bearing the same dedication.

There was a small place of rest and refuge for travellers in the New Forest, then a hazardous part of the country. Little remains of it now, except the name of a fair. This hospital, dedicated to St John near Fordingbridge, was described briefly in the Victoria County History[1] as 'having the usual dedication of town hospitals'. Its administration was under the control of the Bishop of Winchester, John de Pontissara who, in about 1282, appointed its guardian or custos. There was a well known dispute in 1328 between a later warden and his bishop, John of Stratford, who had become involved in the excommunication of a number of laymen, and a powerful laywoman, Joan de Tracy. Eventually its custody was passed by Cardinal Beaufort to St Cross Hospital; unlike much of Beaufort's endowment, this was implemented and, though it declined as a hospital, it remained part of the property of St Cross until modern times. A fair amount of information can be extracted from Bishops' Registers and the archives of St Cross Hospital.

More securely situated was the Basingstoke hospital dedicated to St John which was included in the history of that town by F. J. Baigent and J. A. Millard (1889).[2] It took in the sick and poor, both men and women, and also travellers, but no lepers, except perhaps by mishap. The famous Walter de Merton virtually refounded it c.1340 just before the ravages of the Black Death. It was a small hospital with a chapel and, later, Bishop Fox made it 'practically a home for retired priests'. Apart from Merton, its earlier founders included the Cluniac house of Brownsholme in Norfolk. Henry III became its Royal Protector and the hospital was exempted from the control of the bishop of the diocese.[3] From about 1379 it was usual for the buildings to be leased out, at a yearly rent of 57s. In 1375 it had been leased to the Vicar of Basingstoke, who lived in it with his own household. It was not a fortunate situation; there had to be an inquiry, with the result that the hospital was restored to the Crown by the good offices of Bishop Fox. It was damaged by fire in 1455, but restored, and its chapel was still in use. William Sherwin, a fellow of Merton who inspected it in 1697, described the house as 'low,

ordinary and mean ... the place reserved for such fellows as are dis-
tract and separated from the chief house ... and fit for none but persons in that condition', that is, suffering from some mental distur-
bance. The tenant of the main house had been wanting to pay a
curate to preach once a month. Some remains of the chapel were
still standing in 1819, and the place was described some time earlier
by the younger Dr. Wharton, the poet, whose father had been the
Vicar of Basingstoke. It is one of the most interesting of Hampshire's
medieval hospitals.

* * *

This is a brief account of a number of ancient Winchester institutions, now known collectively as St John's Winchester Charity, and
including one of the city's most famous surviving buildings, St John's
Hospital in Winchester Broadway, north and south. Fundamentally
an ancient charitable institution, it has absorbed many other charities, of which the most famous is Winchester's hospital for lepers, St
Mary Magdalen, on the eastern hill. It is certainly the oldest of the
Hampshire hospitals dedicated to St John the Baptist. For years St
John's has been part of the Winchester scene; the Winchester of the
Saxons, of the medieval world, of the Stuarts, of Queen Victoria, of
two world wars, have all known and seen it fulfil many varied func-
tions. It has provided a school, a chapel, a ballroom, and a meeting
place for the city magistrates, to mention only a few examples of its
multitude of uses. It is still flourishing today, and at a new stage of its
history can surely look forward to many more years of continued
growth and prosperity.

Like all institutions of ancient origin, St John's Charity has been
the subject of varied historical writings, and of occasional reluctance
to discard what is clearly unlikely to be part of the true story. Those
parts of its medieval history written by Dr. Derek Keen are much to
be valued.[1] However, everything written by the fascinating inventor
of Winchester's local history, John Trussell, who died in 1648, needs
to be looked at with much care. Even John Milner treated him with
caution, but Milner valued William of Malmesbury, a writer probably
unknown to Trussell who, fascinating as he was, could not always
read medieval manuscripts.

I must record my gratitude to these Winchester historians of earlier
years, and to Tom Atkinson who first introduced me to Trussell, his
hero. Those who write local history do indeed value each other. We
may not always agree, but how dull Hampshire would be without its
varied local opinions and differing pens.

It was Dr. John Harvey, now of Frome in Somerset, who first showed me the reference in William of Malmesbury to an elderly bishop who had 'Founded an hospital in Winchester'. For that reference, and many years of friendship, I remain grateful. Soon after, a friend returned to Winchester's city library with a large early 19th-century collection of transcripts of hundreds of Winchester documents. Mr. Pepper's wise purchase for the city produced an increasingly complete picture of medieval Winchester.

I must acknowledge gratefully the kindness always shown to me by all the librarians at the city and county libraries. I must also record how much I enjoyed and learnt from my own years as a trustee of St John's Hospital, aided by Mr. Fisher, the porter of St John's South, and his wife the matron. I would also like to acknowledge the kind help of Norman Bower, for many years chief clerk within the office of Winchester's town clerk, R. McCall, and also of my long-suffering editor Noel Osborne of Phillimore & Co. Ltd. Some individual photographs I have acknowledged in the text, but my special gratitude goes to John Crook for his excellent photographs.

We must be grateful to the County Record Office for its recovery of many St John's documents and, in particular, the continued classification of the Rolls begun very carefully by the late J. S. Furley (a Winchester College housemaster). I must thank, too, those kind and helpful members of the Hampshire Record Office, the archivist and her staff, and in particular the two Winchester City archivists Austin Whittaker and Gill Rushton. To the Trustees of St John's Winchester Charity I owe a particular debt for their kindness in inviting me to write this book, and of course I must thank the St John's Secretary, M. I. Jackson, and his staff, particularly Mrs. E. Brown.

Notes

1. *V.C.H.*, vol. 2, pp.208, 209.
2. *A History of the Ancient Town and Manor of Basing in the County of Southampton with a Brief Account of the Siege of Basing House* by F. J. Baigent and J. A. Millard, published by G. J. Jacob, Basingstoke, 1889.
3. Compare St Cross in Winchester.
4. Keen, D., *Winchester Study*.

List of Trustees

As at 23 January 1992

Mr. R. F. J. Steel (Chairman)
Mr. A. Bernfeld
Mr. P. Davies
Mrs. J. Freeman
Mrs. E. D. Hewins
Mr. J. H. Lamplugh
Mr. E. S. E. Lee
Mr. M. P. Lowry
Mrs. M. R. Mussett
Mr. J. Pattinson
Mr. J. Rider
Mr. L. Shaw
Ms. P. E. Starkey

Chapter One

The Hospital of St John the Baptist and its Founder

The Hospital of St John the Baptist in Winchester is one of the most ancient of all Winchester institutions, older than the Norman cathedral, the hospital of St Cross, and most of the parish churches. It lies at the east end of the city, to the north of the statue of King Alfred and near St Swithun's bridge. Its small Norman chapel has survived for hundreds of years, but the name 'St John's' has come to include buildings of all ages: 15th-, 18th-, 19th- and 20th-century. Its modern flats and houses spread along the south side of Winchester's Broadway and along the edge of the River Itchen. Its real estate, houses and shops can be found in many parts of the city, including the High Street, and a new development is emerging from its Southgate Street houses. Another ancient foundation, St Mary Magdalen, is incorporated within its neighbourhood, which forms a widespread and important area of Winchester.

The founder of the hospital was St Brinstan, born in the reign of King Alfred.[1] The 30 years which followed the death of the only king the English people have ever called 'Great' were not years of peace in England. There had been much fighting even before his death in 899. Despite the peace which Alfred had made with the Danes, the Anglo-Saxon Chronicle tells how the King had long ships built to oppose the Danish host. But war was not the only disaster; there was great mortality amongst cattle and men – Walfred, alderman of Wessex and Beornwolf the town reeve of Winchester had both died – and the harassing of Wessex and the Isle of Wight inflicted heavy casualties on the English. Three prisoners were brought to Winchester to appear before the King and were hanged there by order of Alfred.[2]

The city was used to violence, and civil war broke out after the King's death and his burial in Old Minster. He had wanted to be buried in the New Minster, but that great church was not sufficiently advanced for that wish to be carried out, and it was left to his son, Edward the Elder, to fulfil that last desire. The church was completed in 903, the same year that its first abbot, Grimwald, died. There was still no peace in the land, however, and there were dreadful omens: an eclipse of the moon was followed by the appearance of a comet, and then at last, in the year the Winchester version of the Anglo-Saxon Chronicle quotes as 906, King Edward 'from necessity' established peace. In 908 the Bishop of Winchester, Denewulf, died, and was succeeded within the year by Frithstan. More fighting was to come, but even this brief account of the troubles which followed King Alfred's death perhaps does something to show how much his kingdom suffered in the last years of his rule and in the time of his son.

These were years when death and destruction were all too common, and the prosperity of Winchester was always at risk. Even the complicated systems of fortification and defence constructed by King Edward offered only partial security. The casualties of war and the dangers of travel cried out for places offering, if not security, at least some measure of comfort, nursing and temporary peace.

Therefore, it is not surprising that the founder of St John the Baptist's Hospital was an Anglo-Saxon bishop. Brinstan was a worthy successor to the diocese of St Swithun some 28 years after the death of that great man and, like him, was renowned for his piety and charity. He succeeded Bishop Frithstan in 931 when the latter resigned the diocese, and he himself died in 934 after one of the briefest tenures of episcopal office ever to be found in Winchester's long history.

Brinstan was renowned in his own lifetime as a bishop, and during his period of office he founded his hospital near Swithun's bridge and the east gate of the city. He was called holy in the Cathedral Annals and that is the extent of that record's mention of him.[3] It was William of Malmesbury who explained his high standing among the early bishops of Winchester, and Malmesbury may have heard about Brinstan from de Blois's monks, or seen and read some earlier Winchester record. In any case, part of Aldhelm's library survived in Malmesbury until the Dissolution and it is known that William used it. He was his abbey's librarian, collected books for the library and was 'the most enlightened of our historians since Bede'. He had undoubtedly collected a splendid library, and Leland (Henry VIII's historian and topographer) saw some of the surviving books. A later antiquary passing through Malmesbury saw broken windows patched with scraps of ancient manuscripts.[4]

It is unlikely that Malmesbury invented what he wrote about Brinstan, for whose biography the *Gesta Pontificum* is a major source of information. It may be assumed that Malmesbury's story of Bishop Ethelwold's visit to the graveyard of his old minster and how he was addressed by the spirit of Brinstan is correct: 'I am Brinstan, former bishop of this town' he said, and pointing with his right hand added,

'This is Birinus, who first preached here', and holding out his left hand, 'This is Swithun, particular patron of this church and city'. Of course, Ethelwold was impressed, so impressed that he reinstated Brinstan in the Old Minster Calendar, on equal terms with Birinus and Swithun, for this vision secured Brinstan an equal place with these two famous men and 'therefore he should receive equal honour on earth'.[5] His feast day was 4 November and although he was not included in the Roman Calendar of Saints, he was not forgotten elsewhere; in Henry de Blois's Psalter he appears in the Litany, and his hospital was remembered at Hyde Abbey and so recorded by Leland: 'Entering Winchester by th'est gate ther was hard within the gate on the right hand an house of Gray Freres. And hard by on the same hand a little more west is a fair hospital of S. John where poor

syke people be kept. There is yn the Chapelle an ymage of S. Brinstane, sume tyme Bisshop of Winchester and I have redde that S. Brinstane founded an hospitale yn Winchester'.[6] The fact that, in a quotation from a life of Brinstan in another part of Leland, Brinstan is described as founding a 'Zenodochium ante portan Venotanae urbis' simply confirms the other statement.[8] 'Ante portam' does not mean 'outside' but 'in front of', and 'Zenodochium' ('guest house') is not an inappropriate description of the hospital.

There is a brief mention of Brinstan in an early chronicle of Romsey Abbey, but this adds little to Malmesbury's account; its importance lies only in the fact that the Romsey

1. The boundary stone of Lamb's Winchester property at the north end of St Thomas Street, with the Lamb and Flag of St John's Hospital and a punning reference to his own name. A later tenant of the property was Richard Moss.

chronicler considered the story of Brinstan's meeting with Ethelwold to be worthy of inclusion in this 14th-century manuscript.[8] Brinstan also acted as a witness to the granting of Stoneham by King Edward to a Saxon nobleman.[9]

At a very early stage of its history the hospital began to use its own seal, that particular sign of a body corporate. 'Sacred persons', wrote Boutell, 'are usually represented by the emblems associated with them'.[10] So, St John the Baptist was represented by the Holy Lamb and a flag, to be found on a number of deeds which relate to the hospital, and seen today on the site of the former inn called *The Dolphin* at the corner of St Thomas's Street. There are early examples of the hospital's seal in the Selbourne Charters.

A statue of the founder remained in the hospital's precincts long after the Reformation: 'Paid the widows of St John's for dressing the Founder, 1783, usual customs'.[11]

Notes

1. Brynstan, Birstan or Beorstan. In D. H. Farmer, *Oxford Dictionary of English Saints* (Oxford 1978).
2. One of the limited number of occasions when the King was certainly in the city.
3. A. W. G. Sub A.
4. Two Ancient English Scholars, St Swithun and William of Malmesbury. First lecture to the David Murray Foundation, Glasgow, 1931.
5. D. H. Farmer, *op.cit.*
6. The Itinerary of John Leland in about the years 1535-1543, ed. L. Toulmin Smith, (London 1964 ed.), vol. 1, p.270.
7. Leland, *op.cit.*, part 3, p.229.
8. B. L. Lansdowne, M.S. 436.
9. J. H. Harvey, ed., *Oxford* (1969). I owe this important reference to Dr. John Harvey, and was able to publish it in time for *The Churches of Medieval Winchester* (1957).
10. Hampshire Record Society, vol. 2, p.89: grant from Sir Symon de Winton to the hospital, 1285-90. *Op.cit.*, p.89: Lamb with Flag and motto *Ecce Agnus Dei*, 1320.
11. Jacob Scrap Book No. 6, H.C.R.O.

Chapter Two

The Medieval Hospital: St John's before the Reformation

Much of what is known of St John's in its early years comes from three sources: the buildings as they exist today, the hospital's account rolls, and the very important *Black Book* of Winchester, transcribed by F. J. Baigent, whose text was edited by W. H. B. Bird and published by the Wykeham Press, the Winchester firm of Warren, in 1925. This combination of considerable local scholarship at three levels, two of them local, makes it a valuable book, and in the story of St John's it is an invaluable source. The text contains many important decisions made by Winchester's corporate governing body, in no particular order but covering a period of many years. Much of the book is written in Latin or French, and the first entry in English dates from 1441. It is known that the book was handed down from mayor to mayor, and it was clearly meant to be kept in St John's, so it is not surprising that any important document which related to that place, as well as to Winchester's municipal history, was recorded in the *Black Book*.[1] The inclusion of an important document or a St John's entry does not mean that the entry refers only to one matter or one incident; it is recorded because it was a valuable precedent, intended to show how things had been done in the past. Some of these items have small revealing notes beside them – stet or *vacat*, or simply 'cancelled', sometimes just *item* to draw attention to a matter of importance. The order is not chronological: the first entry is the oath, to be said in English, on his knees, by an entrant to the Merchant Guild, the third entry is dated 1477, and the last belongs perhaps to 1418, but the scope of the text is much wider, and provides the most important single historical source for St John's in the Middle Ages.

It may be useful to give a brief account of Winchester's chief archive forms in the Middle Ages, for their keeping was very much a matter for St John's Hospital. The *Black Book* had probably originated in the Tudor need to be more efficient in the keeping of local government records, and to put together the essential documents of Winchester local government, replacing numerous unindexed rolls in simple book form. St John's was an important owner of real estate; it owned more Winchester property than any of the local monasteries, and its property acquisitions had to be recorded in the city on rolls which were cumbersome and difficult to check for particular items. The content of the rolls originated in Winchester's local court, abolished finally in 1835; it was a court of record which meant that its proceedings were of great legal value and could be produced as true evidence in legal disputes. Any private charters which recorded the buying, selling or leasing of real estate, including property mentioned in wills, had also to be enrolled by the court's clerk, eventually known as the town clerk and, to become legal, had to be read aloud in front of the corporate body, or as many as wished to attend, and the court officers, that is the mayor and the two bailiffs. Private charters were kept by the individuals concerned, but enrolments, the copies, remained with the court of record. Legal disputes would be determined by this written evidence of the courts, and its proceedings, all originally noted on small pieces of parchment, often re-used, were carefully copied out onto a roll; that is they were 'enrolled'. Occasionally, the corporation agreed on an ordinance, or resolution, which governed its behaviour on some future occasion unless cancelled. These were important matters, probably always determined by open voting, and it was not easy to find one's way through a series of long unindexed rolls in a search for one particular item.

In the early stages of development of Winchester's local government the ancient and most valuable customs of the city were formed into a kind of collection of by-laws, the *Usages of Winchester*, of which three copies survive, the earliest dating from 1276. One of the items noted as a usage was the order to give 'the Hospital' a free loom, perhaps an early example of setting the poor to work. The usages were continually increased in extent and number in the form of later ordinances on the court rolls. It is obviously a difficult archive form to search. Folios, bound as books, were far less cumbersome and could be numbered and indexed. Thus there evolved the great collection of private charters always known as Stowe 846, named after its catalogue reference number in the British Library, and removed to that library from the collection of the Brydges Chandos family of Avington House when the family were very powerful in 18th-century Winchester. This is the book which has been called the Red Book by Dr. Keene, to distinguish it from its quasi-continuation, the Black Book of Winchester. A book of transcripts was called the Book of Enrolments by the later Mr. Pepper, Winchester's City Librarian, who purchased the manuscript before the Second World War. It is almost certainly in the hand of the great medieval scholar

Dr. Allchin, whose writing can be distinguished in the cathedral library. Another Winchester source which helps to illuminate the hospital's history is the city *Tarrage* of *c*.1417, a taxation roll.

Last, but by no means least, among the written sources for the history of St John's are its own account rolls, a marvellous series which records the hospital's finances and the names of its officers and tenants, and which continues through all kinds of political change, the deaths of kings, the religious reformation, and major changes in the local constitution of Winchester. These are the primary records which depict the changes in the fabric of the buildings, how the hospital was used, by whom it was inhabited and who controlled it.

Almost everybody in medieval Winchester had some need to use St John's, some connection with the place, some reason to be grateful to it. Men and women who were members of the organisation had the right to use it, perhaps as members of the Winchester Guild of Merchants, or of a craft guild. There was scarcely any aspect of public life which did not necessitate the taking of an oath in its chapel; there were obits of friends and relations to be attended. Here the Mayor of Winchester assumed his office, though it was not until Bishop Fox's time that his oath could be taken locally, and the mayor ceased to bear the heavy obligation of making a troublesome journey to find the Exchequer.

Even a brief glance at *Black Book* entries will reveal the importance of St John's in the city's medieval life. It can well be described as a community centre. It was an almshouse, a hospital, a house (*domus*), an inn, and a hospice; it was the meeting place of several Fraternities, of St John the Baptist and of St Anne, including those of the ruling corporate body of Winchester, of the freemen as a whole. The city's archives were kept there, and the city's treasures. Processions began from St John's, like that on St Swithun's day to the cathedral, though the citizens were not always very mindful of that particular occasion. So much went on in St John's in the Middle Ages that it is not surprising that it had to be enlarged once Winchester began to recover from the Black Death.

It is the *Black Book* which reveals that St John's was rebuilt in 1409 during the mayorality of an outstanding man, Mark Le Fayre, a very wealthy innkeeper, whose other major contribution to the Winchester scene was the rebuilding of his own inn, formerly *The Moon*, and henceforth famous until modern times as *The George*. Le Fayre's inn was presumably enlarged with his own money, but St John's was rebuilt with money collected from 'the Friends of St John's' as the *Black Book* calls them; 'the collectors were Gilbert Forster and

Edmund Pycord'. *The George* stood at the south-west corner of Jewry
Street and High Street until it was demolished for road widening at
the end of the Second World War. (In the event, although the road
was widened the scheme for widening the entire western side of
Jewry Street was never carried out.)

The name of Mark Le Fayre is recorded in the 17th-century Book
of Benefactors, a chained manuscript kept in St John's South, but of
much later origin than its form suggests.[2] His only surviving child
was his daughter Katherine who married a London lawyer, Henry
Somer. The Somer's Rentals, among Winchester's archives, record
their substantial estate, but they had no children and all their property was bought by the corporation in 1442. The estate is recorded in
its particular archive and also in Stowe 846.[3]

The list of the Le Fayre tenements in the parish of St Peter in
Fleshmonger Street begins with the one called 'Georges Yn ... occupied by William Benham', and paying the considerable sum of £5 6s.
8d. a year. There was a smaller tenement adjoining it paying 13s. a
year, and it was clearly a substantial addition to the city's income
when, in 1442, the whole estate was bought by the city to help pay
the fee-farm. It had not been hospital property, but it was thought
that some part may have belonged to St John's, and it was therefore
a source of contention and dispute between the hospital's first
trustees and the corporation at the beginning of the 19th century.

***

St John's was a collection of buildings, not one single block, and
from the early Middle Ages consisted of a hospital in the modern
sense, a chapel, and an area where the governing body of the city
could meet; all three places in some respects being interchangeable,
set along the north side of the eastern end of the High Street, and
within a large garden. At the west end was Bukke Street, of which
only a remnant now remains; to the east was the city bridge, traditionally built by St Swithun; to the south lay the buildings of St
Mary's Abbey, and in the later Middle Ages the Inkpen Charnel
Chapel, built partly on hospital land. Other neighbours included the
home of the Grey Friars and the house of the Black Friars. Like the
other two Winchester friaries, these passed eventually to Winchester
College.[4]

St John's could not be described as being in a wealthy part of the
city. There were several small parish churches nearby, and it needs to
be said that the work of the chaplains of the hospital was sometimes

combined with that of these parishes. These churches were among
those which suffered at the time of the Black Death, intermittent
from 1340 onwards. Many closed, buildings fell into disrepair, and
whole streets were deserted, if we believe the complaints of the citizens and the petitions which were continually sent to London plead-
ing that, because of the desolate state of the city, money for the payment of fee-farm could not be collected by the two bailiffs. Not until
1442 was a new charter issued which eventually gave financial relief
to Winchester and allowed the mayor and corporation to buy the
Somer/Le Fayre estate.

When the Charity Commissioners considered St John's at the
beginning of the 19th century, they were confused by its apparent
history and called for its archives. They were referred to a
manuscript history of Winchester written in the reign of James I and
'referred to an authority'. That history was the compilation of John
Trussell. A staunch royalist, lawyer and former mayor of Winchester,
Trussell was an historian whose studies of English history were read
at the universities and indeed became compulsory reading at Cam-
bridge for some students.[5] Like many historians writing in troubled
times, Trussell took refuge in Winchester's historic past, and he was
able to use a number of ancient manuscripts. Alas, the result was not
always accurate and was sometimes very misleading. His inventions
included the 'first' mayor of the city, Florence de Lunn, a misreading from Stowe 846, and John Devenish, the 'founder' of St John's
Hospital, perhaps derived from a misreading of a city 'Charter', a
document which attracted attention through its mention by an earlier
John Trussell. By the end of the 18th century, the story of Devenish
and the hospital had become widespread, chiefly because John
Milner had repeated it in his own *History of Winchester*. The fact was
that Milner refused to accept this story of the foundation and published a definite repudiation of this particular example of Trussell's
stories which he had read in a Trussell manuscript then in the pos-
session of John Duthy, a well-known Hampshire lawyer. Milner wrote:
'It seems plain from Leland that [St John's] was originally founded
as a Hospital by St Brinstan who died Bishop of Winchester and who
was remarkable for his charity to the poor'.

One of Milner's footnotes reads: '... nothing can be more erro-
neous than his [Trussell's] chronology in general'. He pointed out
too that Trussell was wrong in suggesting that there was neither
priest nor chapel at St John's before the time of Henry VI; that there
were rich and powerful members of the Devenish family in medieval
times there can be no doubt, but the story of the foundation of St

John's by John Devenish cannot be accepted, and Milner's own account of the hospital is sometimes confusing. He was almost prepared to accept Trussell's theory of Templar connections with the hospital, because Temple Ditch was a name used for a lane near the cathedral where repairs to the fabric were usually listed in its treasurer's accounts under the heading 'reparationes templi', 'repairs to the temple', i.e. the cathedral.

Trussell's real value is that of a contemporary historian, his works including a long narrative poem about Winchester in the time of the Civil War, and a delightful contemporary account of Queen Henrietta Maria's visit to the city during the time of the plague – the young Queen in her 'chariot' outside the Westgate kissing her hand to the obviously enchanted mayor, 'Adieu, Prefet, adieu'. Trussell appears too as a decidedly bad-tempered lawyer in the city courts, and was at least once suspended from practice because of unprofessional behaviour.

Notes

1. B. M. Add. MS. 6036, and published as *The Black Book of Winchester*, edited by H. B. Bird from a transcript by F. J. Baigent, Wykeham Press, 1925.
2. The Book of Benefactors, also known as The Book of Gifts, 1363-1749, describes Le Fayre as giving his inn to the city.
3. D. May, 'The Somer Rentals in the Winchester City Archives', in Hampshire Field Club, *Proceedings*, vol. 18 (1954), pt. 3.
4. B. Carpenter Turner, *The Churches of Medieval Winchester*.
5. B. Carpenter Turner, *John Trussell*.

Chapter Three

St John's as a Hospital

Like many other hospitals maintained by benefactors, St John's did not admit pregnant women. Childbirth was a fact of life, an event which took place at home, in a palace or by the roadside in a ditch. In this respect St John's resembled the much later Hampshire County Hospital, and shared too the custom of not taking in those known to be suffering from infectious diseases, although smallpox and cholera were unknown in medieval Winchester. Poverty and lack of care because of the absence of a family group were frequent causes of death; plague was usually fatal and malnutrition was rife. It needs to be remembered that removal from one's own home was uncommon. The aged or impoverished parents of the religious in medieval Winchester were cared for in special hospitals attached to Hyde Abbey, St Swithun's monastery, and the third Benedictine house, St Mary's, the Winchester nunnery. Winchester was well furnished with friaries and there were houses of the four orders, but the cathedral in particular could usually produce skilled medical help of a high quality, and this tradition continued after the Reformation.

St John's shared one advantage with the Winchester monastic houses and hospital of St Cross. There was plenty of water, but there does not seem to have been any kind of water-borne sanitation as there was at St Swithun's, and later at Winchester College.

St John's patients were probably the old, the infirm and the childless. Those wounded in the continental wars were generally looked after in the Southampton and Portsmouth hospitals, or simply did not survive the rigours of the Channel crossing. Those who reached St Cross had to endure the further dangers of the road to Winchester, only too well known to early medieval travellers; to go on to London, via the Alton Pass, was a notorious journey which risked a meeting with one of Hampshire's most famous medieval highwaymen, Adam de Gurdon. These hazards provoked one of the best known pieces of early legislation, the Assize of Winchester.

A lonely old age was perhaps the most likely reason for being taken into St John's though, as at St Cross, men were more frequent inmates than women. There is an early glimpse of the life of a hospital patient in the gifts to St John's of Sir Simon de Winton. He pro-

11

vided clean litter (bracken or perhaps straw) for the patients on a regular basis, and a surviving inventory shows that there were also blankets, sheets and bolsters.

The St John's roll, written *c.*1300, begins with an interesting account of the weekly housekeeping expenditure, though the first half of the year has been torn off, and the first complete week of expenditure is for that numbered twenty-six. The chief foods bought were fish, meat and bread; this was for the wayfaring poor. Expenditure on the 'infirm' was accounted for repeatedly and appears to have been spent on the bedridden, those who were more or less permanently ill. They had a male nurse, William de Daxenford, whose salary was 20s. a year. He seems to have been assisted by 'Sybil', whose wages were fixed in kind: she received her keep and an outfit of clothes and shoes at an annual cost of 2s. 2d. Bread in the infirmary cost 33s. 4d. a year, meat 26s. 1d., and fish 38s. 7d. Cloth had to be bought, perhaps for bandages (13s. 10d.) and oil for burning in the hospital. At this point the roll leaves the domestic economy of the hospital and describes expenditure of another kind, the payment of stipends, and the upkeep of hospital property.

The chief administrator was the warden, or *custos*, who was usually in holy orders and worked also as the chief hospital chaplain. He was paid 40s. a year, and there were two other chaplains, one of whom may have been only part-time as he was given only 5s.; the other, Sir John of Alresford, was paid four times as much.[1] The collector of grain in the market received 3s., but that important member of staff, the cook, received three times as much a year. There certainly was some cooking done in the hospital's kitchen, and the larder was rebuilt in the year of this roll, and men were also employed to work on the new chapel.

There is no detailed information as to what happened in St John's at the time of the major outbreak of the Black Death, though the information about the neighbourhood is plain enough. Winchester suffered very badly indeed, even allowing for the customary medical exaggeration. Certainly, at St Mary's nunnery, so near to St John's, the Abbess, Matilda de Spyne, died in May 1349, six months after the plague first reached the city.[2]

It is clear that the hospital frequently received valuable items of plate with which its chapel could be adorned or which could be displayed at the suppers held at St John's on important occasions, though the most useful legacy was, as usual, real estate. An inventory was obviously important, and the items had to be checked and the list handed over to the incoming mayor. The *Black Book* records one actual ceremony, and also the will of the Rector of Michelmarsh in 1494, by which Thomas Smyth bequeathed St John's a valuable cypher 'called a nott' made of silver gilt. It is a unique example of a gift, but the hospital inventory, which had to be produced every year and seen by the mayor, shows the extent of its possessions. One such inventory, 'Its church goodes and all other goods belong[ing] to Seynt Jonys Hopitall', for the year 1441-2 has survived enrolled in the *Black Book*, doubtless as a standard example. William Wyke was then the keeper of the utensils of the house of St John, and was the officer to whom Peter Hulle, mayor from 1431-2, had handed the inventory in the presence of the commonality. First come the chapel's furnishings:

2 ornaments and vestments
2 coporas
4 towels for the altars in the church, good
5 little towels for the lavatory, old
1 Paxbrede of silver and overgylde
1 other Paxbrede
A head of John the Baptist of alabaster
1 box of silver without overglyde
2 chalices of silver with thynne over gelde
1 chalice of silver gylde with owte
2 images of St John the Baptist of alabaster
1 image of our Lady of alabaster
5 clothes of silk and a little pillow
8 partie vestments with all the apparelle
2 surplis feble
1 awte with parurys
1 crystal stone
1 box of divers reliques
4 missals
2 antiphoners
2 porterus
6 salters
2 legends
2 grayells
1 episteler
1 martyrlogie
7 other diverse books
4 sacring bells
4 cruets
2 lamps of brass
1 meat table with 2 trestles

2 bells for the church with trunks weighing 8 cwt.
1 forme

The following items probably relate to the hospital, and not the chapel:

2 meat clothes containing in length 14 yards, with a towel
containing in length 4 yards and a half
2 basins and 1 laver
1 little mortar to pound spices weighing 12 lbs.
4 brass pots
1 belle
1 little posnett
1 hanging laver
11 pairs of sheets
4 pairs of blankets
24 coverlets
1 crowe, 1 spade, 1 shove, 1 howe, 1 rake, 1 spytele
1 dung pick
1 wheelbarrow, 1 bound with iron
1 coffer in the chamber with muniments and charters.

Notes
1. This account is derived from the author's 'Hospital Administration', *Nurses League Journal* (1966).
2. D. K. Coldicott, *Hampshire Nunneries* (1989).

Chapter Four

The Chapel and Hospital of St Mary Magdalen next to Winchester

The Hospital of St Mary Magdalen, 'juxta Winton', once stood on the down still known as Morn or Magdalen Hill to the east of the city and well outside the walls; its extensive buildings and large church making its destruction in the late 18th century among Winchester's chief losses. One has only to consider the potential effect of the demolition of the two other Winchester hospitals, St John's and St Cross, to realise the nature and extent of such a loss.

When the historian Milner first wrote his chapter on the Soke the remains of the church were still standing on the north side of the road on Morn Hill, near the first milestone from the city and opposite 'five ancient barrows in bell form'. The barrows, or tumuli, can

2. The ruins of St Mary Magdalen Hospital, drawn in 1789.

be seen today on the south side of the road, but the remnants of the church vanished between the time of Milner's writing and when he received his proofs from the printers for his edition of 1798. Even Milner saw only 'a double row of naked pillars and arches ... the former ... round ... the latter highly pointed'. He considered that the hospital was founded by Bishop Richard Toclyve at the end of the 12th century, but Milner's chief value lies in his identification of the site; his account of the history of the foundation is faulty. The most recent account of the hospital is that contained in Volume 2 of the *Victoria County History*, but this simply adopts Milner's theory.

In fact, the hospital dates back to an earlier period. It would be surprising indeed if Winchester had not had an early foundation of this kind, as the original object was to provide for the treatment of lepers. A vast number of diseases used to be classed as leprosy, and stringent local and national regulations forbade anyone suffering from 'leprosy' to live within a certain distance of towns or villages.

The hospitals of medieval Winchester provided very effectively for the various aspects of care. At St Cross the aged poor were cared for with residential accommodation, the traveller was given food and drink, and (a much less widely known feature) poor school boys were given a daily free meal. At St John's the poor were also given a home, but the evidence of the accounts shows that medical cases requiring skilled nursing were also cared for, at least until the end of the Middle Ages. Both St Cross and St John's were heavily endowed by private benefactors, as earlier hospitals outside the south and west gates had been. The earliest hospital buildings were much more temporary. They are mentioned in the great surveys of *c*.1110 and 1148 but not afterwards, and were probably used for the accommodation of poor travellers. The only Winchester hospital intended for the isolation and nursing of those with infectious diseases was St Mary Magdalen.

Milner attributed the foundation to Bishop Toclyve, but the question of the hospital's origin was being discussed as early as 1333. In that year an inquiry was held 'in the great church' (that is, the cathedral), and various witnesses called to give evidence. Among them were several prominent citizens of the city, 'Sir Ralph', rector of St Mary in the Forecourt, and Sir John de Tychebourne. It was agreed at this inquiry that part of the endowment of the hospital was an annual payment from the bishops of the diocese of £25 19s. 4d., a grant which originated with Henry de Blois. St Mary Magdalen must, therefore, date from before 1171 when de Blois died. To this evidence must be added that of the Pipe Rolls. As a series, they have survived from 1155 and the earliest show that the sheriff made regular payments on behalf of the King 'to the sick on the hill'. The sum continued as a regular charge throughout the whole of the medieval period. There would appear to be little doubt that it was a payment to St Mary Magdalen's hospital as, when the city of Winchester began to pay its own farm direct to the royal exchequer, the receipt given always includes this 60s. to the hospital of St Mary Magdalen. Moreover, a manuscript, possibly compiled for William of Wykeham's use and containing some account of the hospital's finances, includes extracts from the Pipe Rolls showing these payments 'to the sick' or 'to the lepers' on the hill.[1]

Our knowledge of the hospital in the Middle Ages is very limited, simply because little documentary evidence has survived. The archives may have perished in the disturbances of the 17th century or, perhaps, were never allowed to accumulate for fear of infection. The contrast with St John's and St Cross, both of which have large accumulations of medieval accounts as well as other records, is very marked. A few early title deeds relating to the Magdalen property in the parish of Easton survived until recently in a local solicitor's office, and are now in the County Record Office. There would appear to be no early rental or cartulary. When the Rev. B. Woodward was preparing his *History of Winchester* he examined the Magdalen muniments in the care of the then master, the Rev. W. Williams.[2] There were then only a few original documents with a list of queries relating to the property of the hospital prepared by Richard Wavell when he was master in 1773. This list has long since disappeared and any information about it, or about any of the original archives, would be appreciated.

In the Middle Ages responsibility for the general supervision of the hospital lay with the master. It seems that he was not always resident, and that he sometimes held other offices as well. The most distinguished master was William Waynflete, then headmaster of Winchester College, and later bishop of the diocese. By Waynflete's time (1438) there seems to have been some measure of reform in the hospital's affairs, a reform originated by Wykeham in about 1400. The hospital was apparently poorly endowed, and the two commissioners appointed by Wykeham, John Campeden and Simon Membury, found many 'delinquencies, crimes and excesses'.

The Harleian manuscript No. 328 was probably written at this time. It shows that the hospital provided for seven poor men and seven poor women who were maintained by a small annual sum from various ecclesiastical sources, and by gifts in kind, including old

3. A north-west view of St Mary Magdalen Hospital.

clothes and flitches of bacon. The manuscript includes an inventory of what was in the chapel, among other things a number of books and a 'green carpet powdered with birds and roses'. It is probable that Wykeham's reform, followed by Waynflete's mastership, put the hospital on a fairly satisfactory basis. The decline of the population of Winchester in the 15th century, and of St Giles Fair, were later factors which tended to contribute to another period of decline in the hospital.

Although St Mary Magdalen survived the Reformation, it soon fell on bad times again. Our knowledge of its later history, and what is known of the extent of its buildings, is derived from two main sources: Wavell's *History of Winchester* (1773) and the coloured sketches made for the Society of Antiquaries in 1788 by Schnebbelie and printed as engravings in *Vetusta Monumenta*.[3] A few post-medieval documents have survived and are now in the Trustees Room at St John's Hospital. From these three sources it is possible to put together some account of the later history of the hospital.

In 1545 the number of inmates had been reduced to nine, obviously because it was difficult to maintain a greater number on the hospital's fixed income. Bequests were occasionally received, as in 1611 when the then master, Dr. John Ebden, left an annual sum of £10 to be divided among the inmates, and also arranged for them to have a gown each at Christmas.[4] Very recently a part of Ebden's tomb has been discovered in the office of a Winchester solicitor.

Wavell showed how greatly the hospital suffered in the Civil War. The inhabitants were turned out and Royalist troops billeted within the main buildings. A petition sent to Lord Hopton in 1643 describes the killing of the hospital's flock of sheep, the stabling of horses in the sanctuary, and the burning for fuel of every kind of wooden fitting, including the main altar of the chapel. The master, brothers and sisters had barely returned when they were turned out again in 1665, this time to make way for Dutch prisoners of war. The destruction wrought by these men was greater than that of the Royalists. The fabric was stripped of lead and iron and the new wooden fittings again burnt. Dr. Darel, master in 1671, given £100 by the government instead of the £650 which he claimed, was only able to buy some small properties in Colebrook Street. Here the inmates remained for more than 100 years. The hospital was never reoccupied. In 1788 the remnants of the old buildings on the hill were pulled down, and some of the materials used for the building of the attractive row of small houses known as Rosemary Close, still to be seen off Water Lane.

All possible credit must be given to Richard Wavell, the author of the anonymously published *History of Winchester*, for being the person in recent historical times who took the most interest in the hospital of which he was master. His excellent account[5] is also illustrated by a number of engravings. To these must be added the drawings made by Schnebbelie in 1788 just before the buildings were destroyed. From these sources it becomes obvious that there was once a row of almshouses, in the fashion of St Cross, and a master's lodging.

To the south of the master's house stood the chapel, 77 ft. long and 36 ft. wide. It consisted of a nave with two aisles, its general style of architecture being Early English. The interior walls were decorated with mural paintings on a variety of popular medieval subjects, including St Peter with his keys and the martyrdom of Thomas Becket. The arches themselves were outlined by patterns of bold geometric design characteristic of the Early English period. The chapel must have been one of the most magnificent examples of medieval architecture to be found near Winchester. One of the most interesting drawings in Wavell's History, a page by William Cave, a local artist of great repute, shows the relation of the chapel to the other buildings.

4. Porch from St Mary Magdalen now erected at St Peter's Roman Catholic church, Jewry Street, Winchester.

When the order to demolish St Mary Magdalen was obtained in 1788, Milner was able to save the stone work of the chapel's western doorway. This dates from the Norman period and is thus further evidence for the hospital's early origins. It is now incorporated in the fabric of St Peter's Catholic church in Jewry Street. Today this door is all that remains of the original buildings of a notable local institution.

The name and part of the purpose of the original foundation is perpetuated by the accommodation offered to six Winchester citizens in the attractive group of almshouses on the Weirs, erected in 1929 to replace those at Rosemary Close, as a result of a Charity Commissions Scheme of 1928-9 for joint management of St John's Allied Charities and St Mary Magdalen. By 1984 a large group of additional houses had been added to the almshouses on the Weirs, and they form a feature of considerable merit to St John's Winchester Charity.

Notes
1. B. L. MS. Harleian, and cf. *Black Book*, city account for 1275.
2. B. Woodward, *History of Winchester*, p.242.
3. *Vetusta Monumenta*, vol. 2, plates 1-3.
4. Magdalen Documents: Doctor Ebden's Deed.
5. R. Wavell, *History of Winchester*, vol. 2, pp.155, 211.

Chapter Five

St John's and the Reformation

Early in January 1524 when the Bishop of Winchester, Richard Fox, was already blind and had a suffragan, the corporation let St John's House and its garden to Bishop William Hogieson, Bishop of Darien in Partibus. It was this garden which eventually became the site of the first new building at St John's with the foundation of the six little almshouses endowed by Ralph Lamb, the wealthy client of William Lawrence (or Laurens).

The Reformation had brought its own kind of troubles to St John's Hospital, not because it was a hospital, but because its chaplain was also a chantry priest, and from 1547 onwards chantries were illegal; the Devenish and de Wynton endowments were both objects of government suspicion if they could not be hidden, and though the act against chantries was not immediately activated, St John's was very nearly dissolved like the Winchester monasteries. The cathedral and Hyde Abbey had chantry chapels which suffered. At Hyde the chantries, like the rest of the abbey, were pulled down. In the cathedral some of the chantries were demolished or absorbed into the fabric and used for other purposes, and those that survived were the tombs of erstwhile powerful bishops.

At St John's there was much difficulty. After the act against chantries[1] the hospital and its neighbours, St Mary's Abbey and the Charnel chapel of the nunnery, known as the Inkpen Charnel after its founder, were all threatened with closure, but the city was reluctant to close St John's.

Edward Foster, mayor from 1547-50, and his two bailiffs petitioned the Crown on the grounds that the priest at St John's was not a chantry priest but a hospital chaplain serving the hospital chapel, which was not a chantry. They could do nothing for the Inkpen Charnel and little for St Mary Magdalen. The petitioners claimed that five marks a year had been paid, time out of mind, 'to one chantry priest within the said Hospital [St John's], but in truth there was no priest there'. The King was also asked to decide that the hospital chapel was not a chantry, and that the corporation need not pay any rent for the hospital. The rents which St John's had always had from the Inkpen chantry had already been confiscated, and though the corporation offered to prove its use by the production of 'Olde Annecyent Rentalls and other wrything redy to be shewyd', they clearly were not able to prove their case. The corporation's claims on St John's and to the endowments of the Charnel chapel had to wait until William Lawrence's mayorality in 1554. Lawrence had continued as a Catholic and gained the monastic rents for his corporation, including those of the Charnel, by royal charter at the time of Mary's marriage to the Prince of Spain. St John's eventually passed to the corporation in 1587 as the result of negotiations by another estate lawyer, Edward Cole, but it was Lawrence who helped to bring St John's through the years of religious roundabout after the Reformation and eventually led to the survival of the hospital.

It must have been in the reign of Edward VI that St John's chapel treasures disappeared, together with its liturgical books. The stone and alabaster carvings were thrown into a dust hole where they were seen by Milner in 1788. There was clearly looting going on in the neighbourhood, and there was no-one in charge of the house. It was William Lawrence who, in 1548, appointed a new keeper, or warden, of the hospital in the person of Thomas Martin for 'the good and faithfull service which he hath done in that office of the sergeant shipe ... in so muche as he is nowe aged and impotent'. It was an appointment for life, and Martin was 'to have, occupy and enjoy the custody and keeping of the house of the hospital of St John and the keeping of goods and implements within the same'.[2] In return, the old man received the accustomed fee of 28s. a year and the toll money from Winchester Common marketplace. As a result of this appointment all the minor local officials moved up one grade; John Fludd succeeded Thomas Martin as sergeant, and Robert Foster succeeded Fludd as beadle. Yet it was becoming increasingly difficult to get anyone to act as warden or caretaker at St John's. In 1540 Richard Franklyne was appointed keeper and offered 20s. for the keeping of the house and 18s. for the chapel. He seems to have refused the appointment on the day he was offered it; the corporation at once appointed a priest, William Bartholomew, who was to get 40s. a year and a room in the hospital for the term of his life. He was the last of the priests appointed as warden. By that time the furniture may have been removed.[3]

The Act of Parliament which allowed Henry VIII to dissolve the monasteries did not always include those foundations which could rightly be described as hospitals. St Cross and even the ancient hospital of St Mary Magdalen in Winchester's Eastern Hill were not really threatened, and they continued in much their usual way.

St John's, too, escaped the great Dissolution, and only became vul-
nerable after the enforcement of the law against charities by Edward
VI's extreme Protestant government, who not only decided to pro-
ceed against charities, but also eventually to confiscate all 'church
goods'. The augmentation office had soon discovered the existence
of a chantry in St John's Hospital, said to have been founded by
John Devenish (with the intent to have a priest to sing there, for
ever, to pray for the soul of the founder and all Christian souls). The
documentary evidence is extremely confused, based mainly on John
Trussell's *History* and, as he was the bishop's registrar, the case was
probably made even more difficult by a long-standing dispute which
had gone on for some years between the corporation and the
Devenish family, and also by the apparent existence of a Devenish
chantry inside the cathedral. The augmentation office returns
describe the annual value of the hospital as 100s. a year, of which
30s. went towards the chantry priest's upkeep and 70s. in dispute
between the corporation and the Devenish family. There were also
allegations that the chantry priest had to act as the mayor's chaplain.
Unlike most cities, Winchester does not traditionally have a mayor's
chaplain, and the office may have disappeared at the time of the
Reformation.[4] St John's was somewhat at risk because of the Reformation, and part of its work was to be superseded by the new poor
laws.

The survival of the hospital was due largely to the generosity of
Ralph Lamb and the revival of Catholicism. 'Lamb's Gift', as
described in the will which he made on 17 August 1558, proved to
be the new foundation stone which allowed the hospital to return to
its ancient duties. Here was a man who had survived the religious
troubles of a lifetime to emerge at the beginning of the reign of
Elizabeth I almost certainly a Catholic at heart, and with that most
experienced of legal advisors, William Lawrence. Lawrence, certainly
a Catholic, had survived the Protestant changes of Edward VI's reign
to become mayor in the year of Mary's marriage to Philip of Spain,
and he had repaired the High Cross out of his own pocket in time
for the wedding. Most important of all, he negotiated a whole series
of charters for Winchester with the new government. His patron,
Ralph Lamb, had time to sit for his portrait, which bears the date of
the royal wedding in 1554 and the legend, in Spanish, that he was
the benefactor of men. It shows him dressed in black velvet in true
Spanish fashion, and the picture, on a wooden panel, is the first surviving portrait of a benefactor of St John's. He looks wealthy, self-
possessed, and well able to afford the £400 which he left for his

5. Ralph Lamb, a citizen of London who lived in the capital near Guildhall. He travelled to Winchester for the royal wedding in 1554 and had his portrait painted by a Spanish artist in the latest fashion, black Spanish velvet. (By permission of Westminster City Council.)

executors, Nicholas Charson and William Lawrence, to buy land. This was to be conveyed to the master and brethren of St John's 'wherewith there should be added, relieved, established, founded and kept in the Hospital for ever, a number of poor almsfolk, in addition to those already in the Hospital'. Yearly rents were to be purchased with his money and the money thus granted used for the almsfolk for the said Ralph Lamb.

The arrangements for Lamb's almsfolk were carefully laid down in his will, and were somewhat unusual. There were to be six separate houses or dwellings, each with its own lock and key giving some measure of privacy, maintained by the corporation, who were also responsible for appointing new trustees whenever needed after the deaths of Charson and Lawrence. Each individual was to be given 10s. a quarter and the 'usual feasts'; every other year they were to be given a new gown. Coals to the yearly value of 40s. were to be distributed among them, the distributor being paid 6s. 8d. annually for his trouble. Every year, at the time of the mayor's election, any surplus from the income was to be distributed among the almsfolk at the discretion of the mayor, ex-mayors, and the majority of the aldermen. It was, in fact, a very well thought out scheme, as could be expected from William Lawrence.

Lamb's little houses were built in the inner courtyard of the hospital, in what had perhaps been a garden and, in the fashion of the time, under one roof (a watercolour note of the early 19th century gives the date 1699). They survived well into the 19th century. Although Lamb's will permitted his alms to be given to either men or women the usual inhabitants were poor widows, two of whom eventually gave evidence in the Chancery case which helped to reform the hospital.

So far the hospital had owned property only in Winchester, but Lamb's advisors took the adventurous decision to buy a large estate called Ratfin in the parish of Amesbury in Wiltshire. This had a farmhouse and over 500 acres of land. The purchase required royal assent and permission was also given to carry out the other parts of Lamb's will. Other properties were bought in Winchester, the most important being the substantial block on the south side of the High Street in an area 'bounded by the High Street on the north' and including valuable sites in and around Thomas Street.[5]

The Winchester of Ralph Lamb and William Lawrence was not a wealthy city, though some of its inhabitants were rich. Lawrence was clearly one of the councillors who saw the need for reform in a town where many people were out of work, and where the remedies of the new kinds of poor relief offered only a partial solution. Lamb's remedy was perhaps already old-fashioned when Lawrence carried out his wishes. It was that able lawyer who took the city's charter to London in 1561 and obtained a general confirmation of Winchester's liberties. Neither man had probably yet reached the conclusion that more drastic changes were needed, and that St John's as a whole needed a major reform if it was not to disappear.

On 21 May 1582 the mayor, a lawyer named Edward Cole, called an important meeting in St John's House; the object was to appoint Francis Walsingham, the Queen's Secretary of State and a Privy Councillor, as Winchester's first High Steward, a title of honour paralleled in other cities and intended henceforth to provide a valuable link between Winchester and the Crown. Walsingham played a key part in the negotiations which followed. Lawrence was dead, but Cole, whose task was to negotiate at Court, obtained through Walsingham the Winchester charter of Elizabeth I (finally issued in 1588) which was to prove the basis of the city's government until the great reforms of the early 19th century. St John's House was very much part of this great change, and it is worth looking at the text:

... is appointed the Warden of the Hospital of Saint John by the same name and that they and their successors by the same name of Mayor Bailiffs and Commonalty Warden of the Hospital of Saint John in Winchester may have the perpetual succession and may and shall be in law persons able and capable in all and every manner of plaints and pleas real personal criminal and combined as well spiritual as temporal to plead and be impleaded answer and be answered and by the same name to acquire receive appropriate have enjoy and may have ability and power to possess grant and demise all and several whatsoever the lands and tenements profits hereditaments goods and chattels and rights whatsoever they be and that they and their successors for all time to come may have a common Seal for demises grants and other leases contracts and businesses whatsoever they be between the aforesaid Mayor Bailiffs and Commonalty the Warden of the aforesaid Hospital and their successors and all other persons whatsoever that are to be treated completed and executed And furthermore of our special grace and of our certain knowledge and unaided motion for ourselves our heirs and successors we have given granted appropriated confirmed and released and by these presents we do give grant appropriate confirm and release to the aforesaid Mayor Bailiffs and Commonalty of the City of Winchester the Warden of the aforesaid Hospital and their successors as well all and several the goods and chattels as all and several the Manors messuages lands tenements woods underwoods rents reversions and hereditaments whatsoever and wheresoever within our Realm of England which have before now been granted given or confirmed or are specified declared or designed to be given granted or confirmed to the aforesaid Mayor Bailiffs and Commonalty of the City of Winchester as to the aforesaid Warden Master brethren sisters or any or any one of them or to any or any one of their predecessors by whatever name or the addition of whatever name for the maintenance support or relief of the said Hospital And that they the aforesaid Mayor Bailiffs and Commonalty of the City of Winchester Warden of the said Hospital and their successors shall retain enjoy possess have and peacefully hold all the aforementioned without any hindrance from ourselves our heirs and successors To have and hold all and several the Manors lands and tenements and the other things aforementioned to the aforesaid Mayor Bailiffs and Commonalty of the City of Winchester the Warden of the aforesaid Hospital and their successors for all time to come of ourselves and our successors as pure and perpetual alms willing however that they and their successors shall allow and cause to be allowed out of the aforesaid lands and tenements to each brother and sister of the said Hospital such allowance alms and relief as was used to be allowed in times past We will also and for ourselves and our heirs and successors we grant that the aforesaid brethren and sisters and all other the Ministers and Officers of the said Hospital shall be chosen constituted drawn and in all things governed by the aforesaid Mayor Baliffs and Commonalty the Warden of the said Hospital according to the ordinances and statutes heretofore made or hereafter to be made by the aforesaid Mayor Bailiffs and Commonalty the Warden of the said Hospital according to their sound discretion provided that they be not repugnant to our royal prerogative or the laws and statutes of our Realm of England Moreover we will and by these presents we grant for ourselves our heirs and successors to the aforesaid Mayor Bailiffs and Commonalty of the aforesaid City that this our present Charter being thus made to them as is declared in general terms may and shall be in all things and several of the same force and effect as it would be if all things and several that are above mentioned were expressed more specially legally and particularly in the same our Charter.

Notes
1. 37 Henry VIII. See 'Inquiry concerning chantries in the County of Southampton', p.434.
2. Black Book, p.275.
3. Winchester Charities Inquiry. County of Southampton, pp.3-5.
4. In very recent years, some mayors have appointed a personal chaplain, usually from their own parish.
5. It included the corner site known in the Middle Ages as 'La Peryne', a stone house still bearing the St John's flag with its cross and lamb, put there when Moss was the tenant. It is no longer a public house.

Chapter Six

The Hospital's Chapel 1716-1870 and Dr. Over's School

One of Winchester's most famous physicians in the 17th century was Dr. William Over. He was closely connected with civic life and the cathedral church, for he was mayor in 1675 and his wife Deborah was the daughter of the wealthy Randolph Jewitt, the cathedral's organist. Dr. Over had a successful practice and had acquired a considerable fortune by the time he died in 1701. Unfortunately his wife had died before him, soon after the birth of their third son, the last of three boys who all died in infancy. When the doctor made his will, on 1 April 1701, he left almost his entire fortune to provide for the foundation of a free school for boys.[1] A small amount of money had been set aside so that the members of the corporation might drink a glass of wine annually in remembrance of the doctor, and also to provide for the administration of the income which it was expected would arise from the estate, and which was to be administered by Over's clerk, John Pretty. The chief requirement of the will laid down that the school should provide for a total of 24 boys from the city as a whole, and that two should come from the Soke parishes of St John and St Peter Chesil; all were to be the children of local parents who could not afford to pay for their children's education. The boys were to be taught reading, writing and arithmetic, in order that they could cast accounts, learn accidence and grammar, and thus qualify as apprentices to tradesmen. The mayor and members of the corporation were to nominate the children and appoint the schoolmaster (the only teacher) who was not to be a Welshman, a Scot, an Irishman, nor a north-countryman, lest the pupils acquire 'a vile pronunciation and speak barbarous English'.

Unfortunately, John Pretty fell out with the corporation and was sued in Chancery. As a result of the case, Pretty was ordered in June 1702 to sell the testator's real estate and, after payment of his costs, the money was to be invested for the benefit of the proposed school. The mayor, bailiffs and commonalty, to give them their legal titles, were to provide a convenient room or school house. There were further legal delays, but eventually £570 was invested in a small leasehold estate, known as Goosey Meadow, on the edge of Romsey; the investment produced £22 a year (a not inconsiderable sum) from the tenant, Sir John St Barbe, owner of the estate now known as Broadlands. This arrangement generated an income for Dr. Over's school, but it did not produce a schoolroom until the corporation decided that this would be the best use for the hospital chapel, by this time rarely used, if at all, by the five or six widows living in Lamb's almshouses, and for whom there had been no regular chaplain since the days of the Reformation.

The school which thus emerged as a result of Over's generosity became generally known as the Winchester Charity School, and it remained in the hospital's chapel until the 19th century, when the trustees of the reformed St John's turned their attention to the chapel and to the new forms of state education becoming available in central and national schools.

When the Charity Commission described Over's school, just prior to the reform, they wrote:

> Lord Palmerston is the present owner of the premises charged with this annuity, the whole of which is paid by his Lordship's steward to a schoolmaster who in respect thereof instructs in a room herefore in St John's Hospital (formerly the Chapel thereof), twenty four poor boys in reading writing and arithmetic of whom twenty are of the city of Winchester, two of the parish of St Peter Chesil and two of St John in the Soke: all such boys, as well as the schoolmaster, when vacancies occur, being appointed by the Mayor, Aldermen and bailiffs of the city.[2]

Dr. Over's will was, in effect, being carried out, though there had been long delays in getting his school started, and the legal costs had absorbed much of the money. There were some similarities to another foundation – Peter Symonds' Hospital (Christ's Hospital), effectively opened in 1606; Peter Symonds, Winchester-born but a mercer in London, had made provision for six old men and four young children. Though they all lived in the hospital, there was the same careful provision for the education and apprenticing of the children, and they were kept clean and clothed and by the resident matron.[3]

The school in St John's chapel emerges clearly from the records kept of the place and of the children.[4] The first book is a narrow folio written on vellum and bearing the title 'The Charity School'. It begins with a rather inconsistent and untidy record, and there are scribbles and odd notes – 'Chargals Bond Nr. 1150 in lieu of 4206'. The trustees proved to be highly respected Winchester names, headed by David Wavell, Robert Eyre and Canon Nicholas Preston. Other names follow, all persons of substance: John Penton, Edward Hooker and, followed by the date 28 April 1712, Thomas Godwin, John Vander and William Walter. There seem to have been meetings once a year in 1712 and 1713, two meetings in 1715, and one in 1716, when the trustees included Charles Norton, Robert Eyre and Thomas Cheyney, the last being the then Dean of Winchester Cathedral.

The keeping of more orderly records improved as time went on, and there are regular lists of children admitted and proper arrangements made for clothing the boys. Nevertheless, a comparison with the early years of the administration of the county hospital, founded in 1736, and with Alured Clarke's insistence on regular minute taking, annual reports and the publication of names of subscribers, shows that Clarke's supporters certainly profited from local experience. The organisation of Over's school was of benefit to charitable men of good intent in 18th-century Winchester: they were all learning by their own experience the increasing complexities of what was to become local government.

The first surviving list of 'boys admitted' is dated 12 June 1710, when whoever was present accepted nominations of children by the Bishop of Winchester (Trelawny), the Dean and Chapter, Winchester College, Dr. Nicholas (the warden), and Lady Mompesson, whose nominees included a child of nine, Joseph Dumper, a name later famous in Winchester. The youngest boy was seven, and the other two boys each 10 years and three months. How the school was to be run does not appear to have been settled until 'a general meeting of subscribers' was held on 20 April 1714. By that time there was a treasurer, the Reverend Dr. Erle who, with the Rev. Dr. Braithwait, Mr. Price, Mr. Earle and Mr. Godwin, were 'to act as Trustees for governing the said school'. It was further agreed that the treasurer and trustees for the first years were to fill up 'such places with children as shall become voyd'. No child was to be admitted until his parents produced a certificate from their parish of the register of the child's age, and agreed that the child should continue at the school until he reached 14 years of age.

The rough minutes for Thursday 5 April 1717 fortunately did not prove a model for the school's accounts, which were kept in the early years by a series of treasurers each holding office for a year. The great majority of them were professional men well-known in Winchester, including in the early 18th century such men as William Pescod, the lawyer who built Abbey House, and Dean Cheyney, who made his own fortune and is said to have left 14 differing wills. The school's accounts, meticulously kept, consisted of items which must have appeared comparatively trivial to the treasurers. Each year the

6. The chapel of St John in the Hospital. The two roundel windows, which now adorn the southern side, were given to the hospital by Miss Nancy Kingsmill.

quarterly subscriptions list was carefully added up, and at first there were about 60 annual subscribers. Among them were most of the local clerics whose names can be found on other charitable lists of the time, including those of the County Hospital, and whose inclusion on such lists is only part of the evidence which suggests that the Anglican Church in Winchester was not indifferent to the needs of the poor, though the annual number of subscribers declined as the century progressed. They did not include many of the county's nobility or gentry, for the school was essentially a city affair relying much on local tradesmen who paid their subscriptions quarterly or when convenient for their own finances. Many of them relied in turn on the school as a customer who always paid up, even if it was only once a year, unlike some of the nobility whose bills were often only settled when there was a death in the family. In 1756 the Bishop of Winchester headed the list of subscribers, and his son Chancellor Hoadley also subscribed. Perhaps this may have been because Dean Cheyney was the outgoing treasurer, but both Hoadleys were generous with their substantial incomes and good at supporting charitable causes.

Every year a not insubstantial sum of money had to be paid out for 'mending windows'. Exactly whose windows were so regularly broken by the charity school children gives rise to a good deal of speculation. There were, apart from those in the chapel, many windows belonging to distinguished neighbours, such as the Pescods in Abbey House and the Pentons in East Gate House; the windows of the City Bridewell in the Broadway must have been tempting, but the charity children were certainly not the only possible culprits living nearby. They must have been an obvious target for blame, though not far away were the boys of Mr. Kirby's writing school near St Maurice's church.

The children themselves cost very little to keep. Their shoes were provided or repaired.[5] Their underclothing was more expensive,[6] perhaps made in the school, where the yarn for their stockings was certainly knitted up. What the accounts call 'clothing' was purchased ready made from Mr. Silver for £53 8s.[7]

Educationally the school was well run, with a master and mistress, or quasi-mistress.[8] The master provided the copy books, and presumably ordered the reading books from Mr. Morgan, the annual cost in 1752 being £3 8s. 10½d., much less than the cost of breaking windows. The school-room was heated with a charcoal brazier, and in 1752 there were some special purchases: 'Knapp, pair of bellows', 2s. 9d.; Mr. 'Crompignes bill' suggests the purchase of a clock, or at least a substantial bell, for 11s. 9¾d., or perhaps some maintenance work by this well-known Winchester clock and bell maker.

At the east end of the town in the mid-19th century there were not only shops but inns, including the *Coach and Horses* which was the Winchester terminus of the Portsmouth coach, a silk mill in Colebrook Street and a prosperous stonemason in the middle of what was to become the Broadway. There were frequent civic processions to be watched as members emerged from St John's House with Winchester's three splendid new maces, as well as persistent brawling around the city's Bridewell. There was always something happening near St John's Hospital.

The opening of Over's school in St John's chapel in the hospital produces some interesting observations on the social development of early 18th-century Winchester. In close proximity, in what was later to become the Broadway, was St John's House which was used by the corporation for its annual meetings. These included mayor making and the election of members of parliament, as well as various activities of a social kind, including the first public meeting of 1736, which resulted in the formation of the Hampshire Hospital. Immediately to the east of this public hall, still basically as it was after the rebuilding of 1409, was the chapel full of Dr. Over's boys; behind, to the south, was what had been the home of the Mason family where Elizabeth I had once stayed, and was now the town house of another wealthy family, the Pentons. This was soon to become the truly magnificent mansion of the Mildmays, until the final illness of the Dowager Lady Mildmay resulted in its sale and demolition and the creation of Eastgate Street and many new houses. All these developments simply ensured St John's Hospital's continued importance as a Winchester institution known and valued by a truly mixed society.

Notes
1. R.C.C., 458.
2. Further Report of the Commissioners, pp.258-9.
3. B. Carpenter Turner, *Hampshire Hogs*, vol. 2, Peter Symonds.
4. Winchester City Record Office; *Winchester Charity School Archives*, esp. 214M 35 W/1.
5. Atkinson's bill for shoes, 11s.
6. Michell's bill for linen, £16 14s. 3d.
7. 'Silver's bill for clothing'.
8. The salaries paid varied slightly depending on the small sums of money which had been paid out by either of the teaching staff for any small expenditure.

Chapter Seven

St John's House

Hitherto, changes at St John's had usually concerned the lives of the almsfolk but, in 1751, a handsome legacy bequeathed to the corporation for a specific purpose produced a major alteration in St John's House. It was the rather curious result of political corruption and the influence of the Brydges family, of the great house at Avington, on Winchester life, and of the parliamentary representation of that city in the House of Commons.

Avington was an estate in the Itchen valley which belonged to St Swithun's priory and in 1545, soon after that monastery was dissolved, it was granted back to St Swithun's by the Crown and then passed to a series of private owners including the Clarks, whose striking memorial is in the cathedral. Before 1689 it was in the hands of George Rodney Brydges (who died in 1713) whose mansion house had been exempted from the billeting of troops in 1680. He had been one of the two Members of Parliament for Winchester. His father, Sir Thomas Brydges, had married Anne Rodney of the Somerset family of Rodney Stoke, notorious for their lawsuits. Sir Thomas's son, always known as George Rodney Brydges of Avington, married the wealthy widow of the 11th Earl of Shrewsbury and used her money with great success in local and national politics. His protégés included the future Admiral Lord Rodney, his nephew and godson, who was not, however, as wealthy as his Chandos cousins.[1] When George Rodney Brydges died he was succeeded by his son George Brydges, both as owner of the Avington estate and as Member of Parliament for Winchester, at a time when the city still returned two members. He was an active supporter of Sir Robert Walpole and used his money to further his political cause, helped and urged on by his stewards, Robert Pescod and his son William.[2]

George Brydges first entered the Commons as member for Whitchurch in Shropshire in 1708, and from 1714 sat continuously for Winchester until his death in 1751. For 17 years he 'represented Winchester in his own interest'. In a letter to Walpole in 1734 he wrote 'you are sure of a sincere friend in the House'; in the same year his cousin, the Duke of Chandos, described him as 'a man who had served the administration without any expence to them'. The

money paid out by Brydges to the Winchester voters was distributed
by the Pescods, who were 'the main promoters of the Brydges' cause
in Winchester'. An account book covering the years 1714-59 records
their expenditure and has survived among the cathedral archives as
part of the Pescod papers, because William Pescod was also steward
to the Dean and Chapter.[3]

William Pescod's many posts included the recorderships of Winchester and Portsmouth. It was a Pescod who paid George Brydges'
wine bills and his subscriptions to the county's good causes. William
supported the County Hospital and was its first treasurer and land-
lord, as well as supporting the Over Charity School. Items from his
accounts include 'Mr. Waldron[4] ... for your use – £100', and costs of
his election bills in 1740. The family's connection with the Brydges
had not ended on 2 September 1713 when George Rodney Brydges
had a bad fall when riding and died of gangrene after a bungled
operation on his foot by an Alresford surgeon, 'Mr. Dickens'. The
first Duke of Chandos[5] had paid Pescod £1,500 in 1724 in order to
secure George Brydges' influence for him, thus ensuring that Avington passed to the right person.

It is not surprising, therefore, to read in George Brydges' will,
proved in 1751/2, the reasons for his legacy to the city:

> I give £800 [to the] Mayor, Recorder and Aldermen of the City of
> Winchester, within six months of my decease, with an ... [?] ... that the
> same be laid out in such manners as the Mayor, Recorder and Alder-
> men of the said City for the time being shall think right for the repair-
> ing, improving and advancing their house and building called St
> John's House, within the same City, which I desire them to accept as a
> small benefactory in remembrance of the favours I have received
> from my worthy friends of the said City and Corporation. I give to my
> Steward, William Pescod of the City of Winchester, Esq. the sum of
> £4,000 ...

He had never had any need to worry about his successes at the
Winchester parliamentary elections. The great house at Avington
provided the city with one of its Members of Parliament for many
more years, and the more splendid occasions of Winchester's social
and political life all took place beneath the portraits of George
Brydges and King Charles II in the great room in St John's House,
basically constructed from the two infirmaries.

Brydges' money enabled the roof to be raised and the great room
covered in plaster, with decorative frames of papier-mâché built to

7. The interior of St John's House, showing the decoration which has been revealed in recent years.

contain the picture of Charles II and smaller ones, including that of George Brydges himself, on one side, and later that of Sir William Paulett. The result of the legacy was, as the will called it, 'St John's Room': a large, lofty assembly room in what might be called the Bath manner.

John Milner's description of St John's, published in 1798, is interesting:

... the Hospital had been endowed by Richard Lamb, Esq., in 1554 for the support for the poor widows of citizens, each of whom has a separate apartment in a court on the south side of the main building, the whole being under the patronage and direction of the mayor for the

time being: 'the ancient part of the structure is still applied for the
uses of the corporation'. The principal chamber forms a noble hall,
for public use and assemblies, being 62 feet in length, 38 in breadth
and 28 in height. This was made and fitted up in an elegant style, with
the other offices of the house, chiefly by the benefactions of Colonel
Bridges, proprietor of Avington, whose portrait is suspended in the
said Chamber; its principal object, however, is that inimitable original
picture of King Charles II in his royal robes and full length painted by
Peter Lefoy and presented by that monarch to the corporation when
he became a member of it and had fixed on this city for the ordinary
place of his residence [1683].[6]

In the adjoining room call [sic] the Council Chamber are seen
the City Tables ... disgraceful, for their numerous and revolting errors
to a place that had at all times been connected with literature, as likewise a list of the mayors of Winchester from the year 1184.[7]

Milner's final sentence is most tantalising:

In the dust hole near the apartments of the widows, amongst other
curious antiques, is seen the figure of John the Baptist's head in the
dish, being the bust of the Holy Patron of the house, which formerly
stood near the principal doorway of the ancient Chapel of the Hospital, now made use of for the public as a school.

St John's House was carefully described by a number of local historians, as was the refurbished hall in the Queen Anne Guildhall
which Brydges had also helped to renovate and which continued to
be used for more serious occasions, while St John's saw balls, musical
events and dramatic performances. After the rebuilding of St John's
Room, it became the most important public meeting place in the
city. Here were held the great celebrations after parliamentary elections, when they were contested and the candidates had been introduced to the electors by the mayor in front of the crowds outside,
who had seen the temporary platform erected on the north side of
the Broadway. Subscription balls and concerts became part of
Winchester's social life, and the great celebratory ball which com-
memorated the first centenary of the County Hospital was held
there.

In the late 19th century a series of alterations was made to St
John's House, largely because of a curious change in the trustees'
responsibilities for that part of St John's. It became again much
more of a community centre after the corporation took over the
whole building on a long lease. The city had been presented with a

large collection of stuffed birds assembled by T. A. Cotton. There was as yet no museum in the Square, and the opportunity to display the collection on the first floor of St John's House was too good to miss; it opened to the public free of charge for four days a week. There were occasional lectures and public meetings of various kinds, and the almspeople were always admitted free of charge. The ground floor, which Stopher called the old refectory of the hospital, became a kind of waiting room for travellers using the omnibus services which met passengers in the road outside, and thus it remained, serving King Alfred's buses until recently.

Other major changes took place in the hospital's landowners. Ralph Lamb's Ratfin Farm, near Amesbury, was exchanged for Manor Farm at Thruxton, which had once belonged to the great medieval family of Lisle. Thruxton itself was sold in 1920, and the purchase price invested in Government stock.

Major alterations took place at St John's South in 1974, when some of Brown Carter's buildings were pulled down. There were replacements on the south side, and the hospital was extended on the west with new almshouses looking into Abbey Gardens. The extension, designed by the long-established Sawyer partnership, was opened by the Duke of Gloucester.

In its edition of 10 April 1985, the *Hampshire Chronicle* called St John's House one of Winchester's oldest and most fascinating buildings. It was an excellent narrative, but the account continued with an incorrect description of the great building as built in 1789, originally as the Hospice of the Knights of St John of Jerusalem. An extensive excavation revealed much of the Brydges's 18th-century renovations, and the wall of the great upper hall still showed the outlines of the frames for the portraits of Charles II, Paulett and Brydges in very decorative plaster and papier-maché. During the 20th century the building has had a wide variety of uses, including a period as a cinema, and recently it has become the home of a great exhibition illustrating the Crusades.

Notes
1. David Spinney, *Rodney* (London 1969).
2. For William Pescod see B. Carpenter Turner, *Hampshire Hogs*.
3. Memorial in Winchester Cathedral.
4. The Waldrons were a dynasty of influential mayors; the money was put to good use in avoiding elections and ensuring the choice of the 'right' man for freemen who alone had the power to vote at local and national elections. George Blore, *Winchester*

in the Eighteenth Century, p.19.

5. James Brydges, 8th Baron Chandos, was the head of the family and became the 1st Duke of Chandos. The Chandos archive, with a few exceptions, is in the Huntington Library, U.S.A. The best account of the family is C. H. Collins Baker and Muriel I. Baker, The Life and Circumstances of James Brydges, First Duke of Chandos 1674-1744 (Oxford 1949).
6. Milner, *op.cit.*
7. Both still survive, and are at present under repair.

Chapter Eight

The Reform

Many years after Samuel Deverell's death on 15 May 1849, at the age of 89, his son John wrote the story of the prolonged struggle in Chancery and in Winchester to reform St John's, and his account has not been bettered since it appeared in 1879 as *St John's Hospital and other charities in Winchester*. Since that time, some of the local evidence has disappeared, but John Deverell had worked in his father's firm when much of the documentary material was still easily accessible and in existence in his own office. He was therefore able to write a reasonably detailed account of the various proceedings in Chancery, including the dreadful delays of the kind which Gilbert and Sullivan were able to use with such effect in *Iolanthe*.

There can be no doubt that the chief instigator of the reform was Samuel Deverell, though his son never mentioned this. Samuel was renowned throughout Hampshire as a defender of the poor and a leader of the Hampshire Whigs. He seems to have begun his career as a lawyer in the office of William Faithfull, who had acted as agent for Lord William Russell in a County Election. The corruption so evident in the corporation since the early 18th century had been well known to him. George Earle, a wealthy apothecary, was a leader of the city Whigs, and his very large house in the High Street (No. 105) is a splendid example of late 18th-century architecture. Earle had his chemist's shop on the ground floor, and above were the offices of the Faithfull-Deverell lawyers. To complete the picture, George Earle lived in St John's Street, and Samuel Deverell's home was Colebrook House in Colebrook Street, and this was the headquarters from which he organised the campaign to reform St John's Hospital.

To him and to his friend Richard Hopkins from the Soke, a member of the corporation, the reform of the hospital was essential for two reasons. Firstly, if the corporation's finances were ever to be put in order, and corruption discerned and ended, that part of the city's income which was derived from charitable bequests, and much of which had been administered by the mayor and aldermen since the Charter of 1588, should be entirely devoted to charitable causes. It should not be 'given over to banquets' or other extravagant occa-

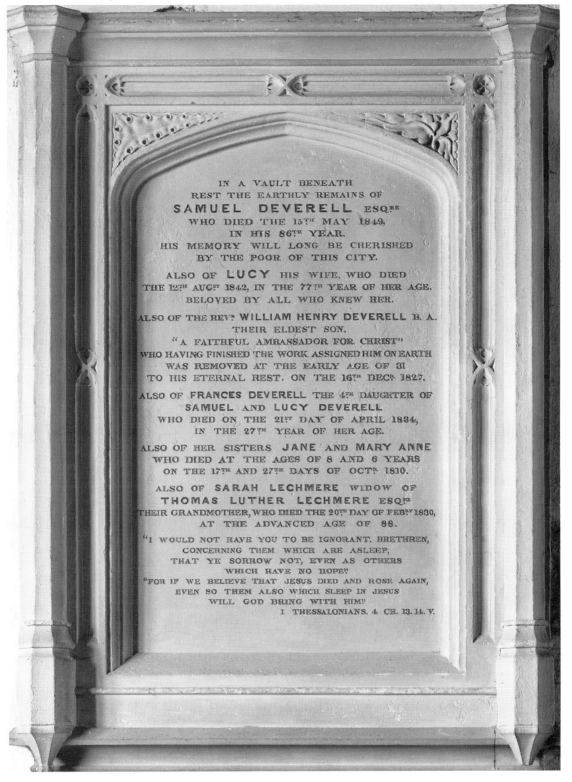

IN A VAULT BENEATH
REST THE EARTHLY REMAINS OF
SAMUEL DEVERELL ESQ.RE
WHO DIED THE 15TH MAY 1849,
IN HIS 86TH YEAR.
HIS MEMORY WILL LONG BE CHERISHED
BY THE POOR OF THIS CITY.

ALSO OF **LUCY** HIS WIFE, WHO DIED
THE 12TH AUG.ST 1842, IN THE 77TH YEAR OF HER AGE,
BELOVED BY ALL WHO KNEW HER.

ALSO OF THE REV.D **WILLIAM HENRY DEVERELL** B.A.
THEIR ELDEST SON.
"A FAITHFUL AMBASSADOR FOR CHRIST"
WHO HAVING FINISHED THE WORK ASSIGNED HIM ON EARTH
WAS REMOVED AT THE EARLY AGE OF 31
TO HIS ETERNAL REST. ON THE 16TH DEC.R 1827.

ALSO OF **FRANCES DEVERELL** THE 4TH DAUGHTER OF
SAMUEL AND **LUCY** DEVERELL
WHO DIED ON THE 21ST DAY OF APRIL 1834,
IN THE 27TH YEAR OF HER AGE.

ALSO OF HER SISTERS **JANE** AND **MARY ANNE**
WHO DIED AT THE AGES OF 8 AND 6 YEARS
ON THE 17TH AND 27TH DAYS OF OCT.R 1810.

ALSO OF **SARAH LECHMERE** WIDOW OF
THOMAS LUTHER LECHMERE ESQ.RE
THEIR GRANDMOTHER, WHO DIED THE 20TH DAY OF FEB.RY 1830,
AT THE ADVANCED AGE OF 88.

"I WOULD NOT HAVE YOU TO BE IGNORANT, BRETHREN,
CONCERNING THEM WHICH ARE ASLEEP,
THAT YE SORROW NOT, EVEN AS OTHERS
WHICH HAVE NO HOPE."
"FOR IF WE BELIEVE THAT JESUS DIED AND ROSE AGAIN,
EVEN SO THEM ALSO WHICH SLEEP IN JESUS
WILL GOD BRING WITH HIM."
I THESSALONIANS. 4. CH. 13. 14. V.

8.   Memorial to Deverell, the first chairman of the reformed hospital, in the church of St John at Soke. He did not want to be buried in a 'smart' part of Winchester.

sions, and certainly not used as a method of political influence, personal patronage and the securing of favourable noisy demonstrations by those who could probably not vote but who might be counted upon to shout -- the Winchester 'Roughs', as a later critic called them. They continued to demonstrate, however, until the secret ballot put an end to the worst abuses of open voting. As in many other cities and small boroughs, the right to vote was limited to a mere handful of freemen, whose membership of the corporation entitled them to call on a number of useful charities, too often used on behalf of their poorer friends, relations and old servants, who could thus be helped financially or pensioned off at no expense to their own pockets. Thus, the reform of St John's was an essential part of the reform of Winchester's political life, to be followed soon by the reform of St Cross hospital, much better known to the general public, though St John's might equally well in certain respects be considered a model for Anthony Trollope's famous novel *The Warden*.

Secondly, and above all, the reform of St John's was the result of that genuine humanitarian concern for the poor which was characteristic of Samuel Deverell and George Earle's successor and cousin, John. Both lived in large houses and were wealthy men, but both lived in a Winchester where charitable help was increasingly based on the parish and around the parish church; where the care of the poor was a parish matter, and a matter for men's consciences; churchwardens and the overseers of the poor had vital roles in this society. The reform of St John's began with the needs of the poor in the central parishes: St Thomas, where the church was still in St Thomas's Street, St Lawrence, St Maurice (then a small medieval church) and St Mary Calendar, where the church had been pulled down in the 17th century, though Methodism flourished on part of its site. St Peter Colebrook had also been demolished, though there were still churchwardens. These parishes were brought to the notice of the office of the Attorney General in a complaint against the corporation in 1811. To the central parishes were joined the complaints of the officers from the very poor parishes of St John Uppe Downe, St John in St John's Street, and St Peter Chesil in Chesil Street. Every parish was represented by one churchwarden or one overseer, and the object was to find out what sums were due to the parishioners for the relief of the poor, what sums of money were received by the mayor and corporation ('the predecessors of the defendants'), whether there was wilful neglect, default or misapplication of any charitable trust, and to ask for the appointment by the court of the proper persons to act as trustees. In fairness to all the various parties concerned, it needs to be said that the object of the application was not only the relief of the poor, but the relief of the local rate payers, many of whom felt that their poor law rates were much too high.

There had been separate parishes within the city boundaries paying poor rates for the churches of St John Uppe Downe, St Martin at Winnall, and St Maurice. St Maurice was an active church, and had long been amalgamated with the closed church of St Peter Colebrook and St Mary Calendar (excavated in 1989) in the north High Street. A very large number of ratepayers in central Winchester found it to be in their financial interest to try to reform the existing parish arrangements for the relief of the poor and pass the burden over to St John's Hospital if the nature of the hospital's endowments could be discovered and taken away from the corporation. It was all too easy to think that hospital income was being wasted on riotous living, and even on bribing the electors. That there had been bribery at national and local elections there was no doubt, but most of the money for bribes appears to have come from private sources.

The application by the Attorney General had many supporters for many reasons, and the case for reform was strengthened by a second Chancery suit begun by the Attorney General on the same day, 21 March 1811. This second case was an example of the detailed knowledge some of the reformers had of the property the hospital once possessed. Both Elizabeth Good and Elizabeth Pyott had married into well-known Winchester families. The Goods had been lawyers, deputy High Sheriffs, while the Pyotts were Quaker philanthropists. They were large families who extended through the social scale, and had very varied financial fortunes, resembling in this respect the Wavells and the Pentons. Mrs. Good and Mrs. Pyott, on behalf of the other poor sisters living in the hospital, were the nominal plaintiffs in this second Chancery case against the corporation, asking for details of the hospital's estates and the income thus derived which ought to have been received by them. If misuse or misappropriation was found, then the court was asked to recover the monies on behalf of the plaintiffs and to appoint trustees for the future.

The two suits began on 21 March 1811 but neither was determined until May 1817, by which time the original plaintiffs were dead, but the decrees made were still only decrees *nisi*. Nearly a year went by before they were made absolute in January 1818, but there had yet to be further hearings by two masters before all the matters were consolidated into one cause and a report made in April 1823. The only doubt left at this stage was as to who owned *The George*,

claimed by the corporation and also the hospital.[1] It was necessary
for the reformers' lawyers to prove in Chancery the hospital's title to
every piece of real estate. So, on 2 August 1825, the British Museum
trustees produced their manuscript of the Winchester *Tarrage*, which
clearly indicated the difference between corporation and any original hospital ownership of property.[2] This was a decisive point in the
case, but another major hurdle remained: the royal charter of Elizabeth I had given all this property to the hospital, and an Act of Parliament might be needed to take it away. There were further reports
and appeals in 1826 and 1827, and a compromise was suggested in
1828, but in July of that year, when the master hearing the case
decided that the properties had been vested in the corporation by
the 1588 charter, it was clear that an Act of Parliament was necessary,
and the Lord Chancellor confirmed this suggestion. At last, on
24 June 1829, the Royal Assent was given to this private act, an act of
enablement which allowed the corporation to convey their hospital
estates to new trustees appointed by the Court of Chancery.

It had taken 18 years to ensure the future of St John's, but once
the act had been passed matters moved fairly quickly. The corporation of Bristol was able to hand over Thomas White's benefactions,
and the new trustees could buy new almshouses, grant 90-year leases,
and appoint new trustees should the occasion arise.

The act of June 1829 needs to be seen against the background of
the general demand for social reform which was such a feature of
English society in this period, and its application was made possible
by reformers in Winchester. It covered every aspect of what was
required to set up a governing body of trustees with full powers to
govern the hospital and its allied charities. It had obviously seemed
important to choose trustees whose social and financial status was
such that the disinterested administration of the charities could not
be in any doubt. On 2 August 1830 the first new trustees were
appointed, 13 in number and headed by the Bishop of Winchester,
Charles Richard Sumner, the headmaster of Winchester College, the
Rev. David Williams, and the Rev. Harry Lee. These three
redoubtable churchmen were followed by two county gentlemen,
George Lowther and the Rev. Gilbert Wall Heathcote. Lowther was a
Wykehamist and the bishop's tenant at Wolvesey Palace from 1828;
he had married Warden Huntingford's niece.[3] Heathcote was a
member of the well-known family of Hursley. Next came the professional men whose standing and integrity was deemed to be beyond
doubt: Henry G. Lyford,[4] the famous surgeon from the County Hospital, Samuel Deverell, the leader of the reformers, and his colleague

9.   The courtyard of St John's North as drawn by Prosser.

Richard Hopkins, who had been expelled from the City Council apparently for his association with reform. John and James Young were reformers in local government, and John was to be the first 'reformed' Mayor of Winchester, though he died soon after his appointment as a trustee. John Harvey, a draper from the Square, James Woolly and Benjamin Ford were all local tradesmen.

The first volume of the Trustees' Minutes, recording their quarterly meetings, begins on 14 October 1831 and ends on 16 October 1877. At the first meeting the Bishop of Winchester and his tenant, Lowther, were supposed to nominate for Symonds Charity, but they were not present and the other trustees filled the vacancies with two women, Sarah Ireland, aged 63, and Martha Richards, aged 68. Other places were allocated, the oldest nominee being 88, and the orders for future nominations were decided.

The reformers soon gave careful consideration to the need for new almshouses. The only accommodation was the small group of buildings of 1699 originating with Lamb's bequest, added to the Tylney's gift on the north side of the High Street in the courtyard. This was formerly the garden behind St John's House, and provided no room for expansion. St John's North, the architect of which was Henry Carey Brown,[5] consisted of 22 almshouses on a limited site. All around lay the outbuildings and the gardens, including the famous lawn of the Pentons' great town house, which was by this time in the hands of the Mildmay family. The dowager Lady Mildmay visited the city regularly, where she was greatly loved, and the family were much involved in local politics. Winchester College was another adjacent owner, and Eastgate Street did not yet exist.

St John's South

The only chance to expand the hospital was for the trustees to buy a suitable site at the south-east end of the High Street, where there were less powerful owners and occupiers who might be persuaded to sell. The area had long been occupied by stonemasons and a builders' yard, though it had been greatly improved by the construction of a new bridge over the Itchen in 1813, designed by the cathedral's surveyor, George Forder. Forder's contemporary at the cathedral, William Garbett of Portsmouth, was already well known throughout Hampshire and in Winchester where he had been appointed the first permanent cathedral architect of modern times, though the Dean and Chapter with its considerable estates had long had land surveyors. It was Garbett's misfortune to coincide at the cathedral with George Frederick Nott, a very wealthy canon who considered himself a good architect and who moved the memorials and tombs. He also replaced the cathedral's medieval Decorated style with his own form of 'Norman' architecture in the north transept. Poor Garbett also had to deal with John Nash, who was called in to advise about the repair of the nave pillars with eventual disastrous results, as the work was carried out with cast iron.[6] Nevertheless, Garbett's practice in Winchester and Hampshire was important and influential, but his health was already undermined when the trustees met on 14 October 1831 and instructed him to report on the premises occupied by Mr. William Redstone at the east end of the High Street.

At the November meeting of 1831, Garbett was asked to 'furnish plans of the premises'. When they next met, on 31 December 1831, they decided not to spend more than £100 on new almshouses, but that it was expedient to erect a room there for the transaction of the business of the hospital and of the various charities, and for the keeping of documents. No further meeting was held until 7 April 1832. In due course Mr. Redstone was given notice to quit, but there were two important interests in the property which had to be purchased: those of Lady Mildmay and Mr. Martin Filer. Filer was a well-known builder, whose family had for centuries been tenants of the Dean and Chapter in Droxford, where they owned the paper mill. The eldest sons of the family were always called Martin, and the funeral of the last Martin in the mid-19th century was a famous Winchester occasion.

Any owner on the south side of the roadway had to be bought out before the construction of what was soon to be known as St John's South could be approved by Chancery. The death of a trustee, James Young, also caused some delay, and it was not until 4 March 1833 that the agreement to purchase 'the site of the Hospital' was eventually concluded with Mr. Filer. Garbett's plans and specifications were not ready to go to Chancery until they were approved at the meeting on 20 May 1833, and then on 2 October 1834 William Garbett's death was reported. That the building was well advanced seems clear, and at the same meeting Mr. Owen Brown Carter, who had been born in London and had worked in Garbett's office, was appointed to succeed him 'in superintending the completion of the building'. He was to be paid a proportion of the commission of '5% of such building as agreed to be allowed'.

There was a further meeting on 29 January 1835; the work of building St John's South went on very quickly, and the trustees soon had spare places for new almsfolk which were rapidly filled. They were keeping a careful eye on the building work and particularly, one imagines, looking at the hall and room 'for the business meetings of the Hospital and other charities' and for keeping deeds and other records. In April 1832 David Williams had been an occasional chairman, but the real work of reform was done by Samuel Deverell. For many years there were no sub-committees, and historically it is a loss that when they were formed their minutes were apparently destroyed.

St John's South is the best surviving Winchester example of the work of William Garbett and his young draughtsman Owen Brown Carter. It was a new style of architecture, using materials which broke away from the plain designs in red brick with classical windows and columns which made the buildings of Georgian Winchester so distinguished and which are still so pleasing to the eye. The new Corn

Exchange in Jewry Street won an architectural competition for Owen Brown Carter. The prize was £16, but it spread his name to many Hampshire gentlemen, including the Baring family, and to wealthy clergy. It was built in a kind of London stock brick with a classical portico, and was soon followed by another distinguished rebuilding, that of the new Trustees Savings Bank at the south-east corner of the High Street and Southgate Street, which had unusual brick and stone windows of interesting perspective in his Egyptian style. Owen Brown Carter belonged to that period in architectural history when the difference between architects and surveyors was beginning to emerge very distinctly, and when many of the talented architects of the period were friends of gentlemen with wealth and taste and had travelled abroad. Brown Carter himself had been to Egypt.

It was Brown Carter who finished Garbett's rebuilding of St Maurice's church, which replaced a little medieval church with a new High Street frontage, and where he used the same kind of grey headers placed to such advantage in St John's South. The decision to build St John's South had been taken long before St Maurice's church was completed, but when at last it was it proved an impressive addition to the High Street: its Norman tower had been retained, as well as the ancient passageway beneath which was not a right of way. St Maurice's and the addition to the hospital, with their combination of stone, flint and grey headers, were to prove much more pleasing High Street buildings than the Guildhall which followed some 40 years later.

Brown Carter is known to have lived in a classical-style house in Southgate Street while designing much of the great terrace on the south side. This terrace is used as extra accommodation for St John's Hospital, but was once in demand by army officers, since they were near the barracks, the cathedral and a new parish church, St Thomas, with a popular evangelist preacher, Canon Carnes. Brown Carter's work included several churches: St William's at Otterbourne, where his patron was William Yonge, and the church at Amesbury in Wiltshire where the author once saw a faded copy of Brown Carter's plans displayed in the porch. The cathedral's choir pulpit and some of its chairs show the quality of the work he could achieve in church design, but it was left to his pupil from 1841-4, G. E. Street, to restore and renovate St John's chapel, a task which was not given to Thomas Stopher. Despite Stopher's interest, his work there did not amount to much more than maintenance and the dormer windows.

10. The entrance to St John's South viewed from the Broadway.

11. The interior courtyard of St John's South.

At St John's South, Garbett and Owen Brown Carter produced a group of almshouses clustered round a central space, and with their gables and barge boards they formed a traditional almshouse group, for all their use of unusual materials. The gabled gatehouse is the central feature of the wing which frames the High Street frontage; it is built in stone with grey headers and is tile-hung. The well-proportioned mullioned windows, and the fact that each house was built as an individual dwelling, produce an air of comfort and cosiness, of buildings designed for a specific purpose. The covered passage which links the buildings on the south side adds to this feeling; neighbours can visit each other in comfort, and in the wettest weather. Over the gateway Brown Carter designed what came to be called the board room, where the trustees met, and there is an interesting period fireplace, and a majestic wall-safe for the custody of the hospital's documents, all as specifically ordered. The fireplace is topped by a 17th-century chimney-piece, placed there by a later Winchester architect, Thomas Stopher, who moved it from Amey's Coffee House, a St John's property which was demolished by order of the trustees. This had been a kind of teetotal restaurant on a small plot behind Lloyd's Bank, and its site is represented by the gap in St Thomas's Street still visible today.

The whole building does much credit to both architects, and William Garbett's memorial in the cathedral's south transept provides a fitting postscript, a generous but justified tribute designed apparently by the younger man. Garbett was buried in old St Thomas's church as 'a zealous and faithful servant to the Dean and Chapter'. The fact that Brown Carter designed fittings only for the cathedral and St Cross hospital can be explained, sadly, in terms of his misfortunes in later life. His only child, a son, died in South Africa, and he himself turned to drink. He may have designed *The Green Man* on the corner of St Swithun's Street, perhaps too near to his own house. He died in poverty in Salisbury in 1859.

Later Changes

In 1844 new arrangements for leases were made to end the need to apply to Chancery for every individual property. One of the first leases to be granted was of Clifton Hall, of three acres, where a local builder, a Mr. Newman, built an attractive terrace of houses; after the lease fell in 1906 the income rose to about £11,000, and in more recent times the houses have been sold to private owners. They form a most attractive addition to the Winchester scene.

12. The new riverside block of St John's South. MARY MAGDALEN.

13. The interior courtyard of St John's South.

14. A characteristic photograph of Miss Emily Firmstone, the first woman trustee of St John's Hospital, who was well known throughout the city for her energetic support of many charitable causes. (By permission of Hampshire Record Office.)

Soon after the reformed St John's had been established under its first trustees, a new kind of small quarterly magazine was founded by a printing press in College Street (and later behind the City Cross) under the editorship of its owner, William Tanner. It was called the *Winchester Quarterly Record*, cost two pence, and along with its editor soon became known for its Christian evangelical tone.

In 1851 the Dean was the 'Highly Respected and Truly Liberal' Thomas Garnier, and St John's House was offering a wide choice of entertainment to a public predominantly of his political opinion and deeply interested in opportunities for every aspect of education. M. Gompetz exhibited his 'Great Panorama of the Arctic Regions' on 11 September 1851, and Signore Malagarini gave an evening concert at St John's House which was 'fashionably attended'. It was an exciting evening; the band of the First Royals played and members of the cathedral choir sang. As autumn approached there were other activities. The Mechanics' Institute began its courses of winter lectures, beginning with an evening devoted to the 'Music of England'. The Charitable Society of Natives held its annual dinner at the house, presided over by a prominent Liberal member, John Bonham Carter. With the approach of an election, all three candidates dined there with the British Order of Foresters on 5 July; all candidates made speeches at the 'evening with a Ball'. On 7 July, nominations took place in St John's, all being made in public and announced to the assembly outside by the mayor, Mr. Charles Mayo, a famous surgeon at the County Hospital. After a show of hands, a poll was demanded for the next day, with the result that the citizens returned one Conservative, J. B. East, and one Liberal, John Bonham Carter. There had not been an election for some years. All the shops closed but, as reported in the *Record*,[7] 'The Public Peace was not disturbed'.

The last half of the 19th century saw much architectural change in Winchester and the demolition of many of its 18th-century houses. Not all of this new architecture has been considered by modern eyes to have been of a very high standard, although much was the work of Thomas Stopher, surveyor to the trustees of St John's Hospital. It is not surprising that much of St John's property helped to change the face of the city. Stopher's notes on Winchester buildings, left in manuscript form and now in the Jewry Street library, are particularly valuable, not least for his comments on Winchester personalities. He clearly made a great architectural impression on the city and was a loved and valued mayor.

In 1894 there were 12 trustees, of whom eight applied to the Charity Commissioners for a new scheme and additional trustees. Under the new scheme there were to be 14 trustees: two councillors for the ward of St John, six trustees elected by the City Council for three years, and six corporate trustees each appointed for eight years, whose appointments were to be approved by the Charity Commissioners with, in addition, the mayor of Winchester *ex officio*. There were to be new arrangements for letting properties, in particular for the letting of farm leases. Property was no longer to be let on beneficial leases, but on rack rents, as annual tenancies or short leases. Tenants had to be responsible for their own internal repairs. These arrangements proved particularly beneficial, and the example quoted by Stopher[8] concerned the attractive group of houses called Clifton Terrace on the Western Hill, let for £36 a year ground rent. 'In 1816 this was a field', and was included in *The Further Report on Charities*:

> 2 – A piece of land without Westgate, containing between two and three acres, now held by Bryant Wickham Holloway, together with a close called the Arbour, belonging to the Corporation, by lease, granted in consideration of a fine of 10s. for 40 years from Lady-day

1806, at the yearly rent of £2 1s. 6d. for the whole and 2s. 6d. in lieu of capons. The annual value of the piece of arable land is stated to be about £5. In order to account for the smallness of this fine and rent, in proportion to the value of the land, it is stated, that the lease contained a covenant from the lessee, to permit an annual sheep fair to be held on the field called the Arbour; and that the people of Winchester claim a right to use the Arbour as a playing place, which right is reserved by the lease; but neither of these circumstamces ought to have lessened the fine or the rent payable for the arable field derived from this donor's gift. It appears to us very desireable that in all cases the property belonging to the charitites should be let distinct from that of the corporation.

Notes

1. In fact it belonged to the corporation through the purchase of the Somer's estate. Nor was it yet clear who really owned the Guildhall. The 'Assembly of the Four and Twenty' was called together on 7 November 1823 by the then mayor, Charles William Benny; the meeting resolved unanimously 'that the writing down of the corporate property be instituted to discover whether the Town Hall is not the property of the corporation, and that the material remonstrance of the strongest kind be made to the Trustees of the Charities against the repeated claims set up by them on the ground of the express understanding that the compromise entered into with the relators on purpose to end all further litigation'. W.C.R.O., W/B2/12.

2. The manuscript (B.L. Add. MS. 6133) still bears the note 'this book was produced and shewn to Henry Godwin [and] is the same book referred to in his affadavit, James Ralfe, Master Extra in Chancery, 2 August 1825'.

3. See Hilda Stawell, Warden Huntingford.

4. See B. Carpenter Turner, *Hampshire County Hospital*, passim.

5. Unfortunately, his carefully designed corner house further west, built as his own residence, was recently demolished; it had ruined the architect financially, and left him poor enough to be taken into St John's himself as an almsman. He was Thomas Stopher's father-in-law.

6. Quarterly Record.

7. August 1851.

8. Thomas Stopher, Further Report on Charities (1924).

Chapter Nine

St John's Charity: The Modern Charity

The charity is now one of the most significant independent housing organisations in the city of Winchester and currently provides accommodation for 90 elderly people in 76 housing units. In addition, the charity will shortly be opening a 20-bed extra care unit for the frail.

The old Victorian almshouses on the north side of the Broadway, St John's North, have all been fully modernised and many converted into one-bedroom flats. In 1974 the new development on the south side, St John's South, provided an additional 20 new flats. The St John's South development was financed with assistance from the City Council in the form of a mortgage, and the Mary Magdalen development with a Housing Corporation loan.

It can rightly be claimed that almshouse accommodation was really the forerunner of modern sheltered housing. The charity has, however, evolved a system of care and support for its residents which exceeds much that is offered in many private and council sheltered schemes. For many years the charity has had a policy of employing qualified nurses who are called matrons. They perform the role of wardens, but because of their nursing qualifications can provide a greater degree of support to residents than the wardens found in many sheltered housing schemes. They are able to provide nursing assistance in an emergency and, subject to arrangements with the residents' doctors, nursing care during short-term sickness. Their nursing skills are also invaluable in helping residents generally when trying to cope independently during the onset of physical or mental frailty.

The charity's welfare staff currently consists of a matron and her deputy and assistant. Generally these are all resident, although there is currently one non-resident matron. The almshouses are all linked to the matrons' accommodation by an emergency alarm system and 24-hour cover is provided. In addition to the matrons, the charity employs a part-time care assistant who helps some residents who have difficulty bathing. This generally takes place in a specially equipped bathroom fitted with a Parker bath, a medical bath with easy access and a hydraulic tilt mechanism. Adjacent to the bath-

15. & 16. St John's North. The architect was Henry Carey Brown.

room is a room where hairdressing is provided once a week. It is hoped that a regular chiropodist's session will also start there shortly. The final member of the welfare staff team is a domestic assistant, who helps a number of the more house-bound residents by doing their shopping and collecting their pensions.

The charity's growth in recent years has increased administrative responsibilities, and it now has a full-time General Secretary supported by an administrative assistant, a part-time accountant and an accounts clerk. The charity also has its own maintenance staff of five full-time employees, together with a full-time gardener. The Secretary is directly responsible to the Board of Trustees which has overall responsibility for the management of the charity. It currently comprises nine trustees, one of whom is nominated by the Bishop of Winchester, three by the Winchester City Council, and the remaining five are co-opted.

The ethos of today's almshouses is centred on belief in St John's as a community rather than an institution. While it provides as comprehensive a network of care as possible, all residents are encouraged to live as independent a life as they can. The growth of the charity in recent years means that it is big enough to have a positive identity of its own, and being part of this community is one of the central attractions of becoming a resident of St John's.

The charity's links with the Church are important. The chapel in the Broadway is still, after so many centuries, a place of regular worship. This, as much as anything else, symbolises the continuity of St John's, and chapel services provide a focal point for community life. It is extra-parochial and the trustees employ a part-time chaplain who conducts regular services and provides pastoral support for residents.

Since the introduction of the first charitable schemes after the great court case of the 19th century, admission of residents has been based on an assessment of need. Today's Charitable Scheme states that residents must be 'needy persons of good character'. Consideration of applications is a key responsibility of the trustees and is not an easy task. All applications are carefully scrutinised, and when a vacancy occurs it is filled by appointing the person felt then to be most in need of the accommodation. This means assessing applicants' financial resources, but also their housing social needs, in the sense of their need for the care and support offered by the almshouse welfare staff.

The charity has been fortunate in benefiting from the boom in city-centre rents which has taken place in recent decades. It is a

17. & 18. St John's almshouse residents past and present.

popular myth in Winchester that St John's owns much of the High Street; in fact, in the last 20 years or so, the investment property owned by the charity has been rationalised and reduced. Many residential tenancies were sold off and the proceeds used in the refurbishment of key offices and retail property. The charity's current portfolio of investment property means, however, that it has a significant rental income which remains its main source of revenue. The charity's income has allowed it in recent years to consolidate the housing it provides. It has also meant that as well as supporting all the current activities and running costs of the charity, by judicious management the trustees have built up reserves to fund new development.

Just over three years ago the trustees resolved to pursue the idea of providing an extra care unit for the frail. In doing so they were responding to new pressures facing all those engaged in the provision of care for the elderly. As more people live longer, so an increasing number live to an age when independent living ceases to be possible. This results in the need to make a move late in life to residential or nursing care. Such moves are always traumatic, and all the more so when they involve moving to a completely new setting, and the concept of the charity providing such care itself was something which commended itself to the trustees. Careful thought had to be given to the form of such a unit. Although there are a growing number of such schemes in the country, the term does not always encompass the same concept. It can mean sheltered housing with extra support, residential care, nursing care, or a combination of these. It is the latter, a 'dual registered' home, that the trustees resolved upon after careful appraisal, so as to ensure maximum flexibility in the care provided.

In 1984 the existing charitable schemes governing the operation of the charity were consolidated. Indeed, it was at that time that the slightly cumbersome title of 'St John's Hospital and the Allied Charities with which is united the Hospital of St Mary Magdalen' gave way officially to 'St John's Winchester Charity'. The advent of extra care meant some revisions to the 1984 Charitable Scheme which were incorporated by an amending scheme in 1988. This empowered the trustees to convert one of its investment properties, the *Winton Court Hotel* at No. 49 Southgate Street, into an extra care unit for the frail elderly. After discussions with the Charity Commission it was agreed that the charity could admit residents directly into the extra care unit, but priority would be given to existing residents of the almshouses.

As the final pages of this book are being written the charity is approaching the end of a three-year development project to convert the *Winton Court Hotel* and, at the same time, refurbish the adjacent office premises as Nos. 41-47 Southgate Street. The extra care unit has been named after John Devenish, whose name has been closely linked with the charity over the centuries even if, as early chapters have indicated, he is clearly not the founding father he was once thought.

19. Devenish House, Southgate Street, the latest addition to St John's Hospital.

Devenish House will have 20 beds and will provide 24-hour residential and nursing care. The building, designed by David Yearley of local architects Plincke, Leaman and Browning, is an innovative combination of the old and the new. Owen Brown Carter's front façade is preserved, while to the rear a modern extension provides attractive residents' rooms with inverted bay windows giving each room a balcony. A striking feature of the building is its conservatory lounge which looks across the roofscape of Winchester towards St Catherine's Hill.

Although Devenish House is a little distance away from the charity's existing almshouses, every effort will be made to integrate its residents into the community of St John's. Likewise, despite the increasing frailty of its residents, the charity will seek to foster as homely an environment as possible and to avoid the building becoming too institutionalised. It aspires to be a place where people 'live' rather than where they are 'taken care of'.

In 1989 a service of thanksgiving was held in Winchester Cathedral to celebrate over 700 years of the charity's role in the city. As 1289 had so often been recorded in prior histories as a foundation date the trustees chose to recognise 1989 as an anniversary year, even though modern research has revealed the much earlier origins of the charity. The development of Devenish House today echoes the aspirations that must have prompted the foundation of its medieval forerunner in the hospital at St John's House, and makes it an apt commemoration of the past as well as a reminder of the charity's adaptability to the needs of the present and, indeed, the future.

Of the future, it can be said that even now the charity is looking to extend its role yet further. Plans are being discussed for the charity to assume responsibility for two other smaller almshouse charities in Winchester: Christ's Hospital and D. K. Murray's Charity. The former is part of the legacy to Winchester of its famous 17th-century citizen, Peter Symonds; the latter the testamentary creation of an early 20th-century mayor whose name the charity bears. The plans currently being discussed offer these smaller charities the benefits of amalgamation with a much bigger organisation, with its broader financial base and a full- time administration. Every effort will be made to preserve the individual identity of these historic almshouses, as has already been done in the case of the hospital of St Mary Magdalen. The charitable scheme implementing such an amalgamation will also extend the charity's trusts to allow its trustees to apply surplus income to the relief of need generally, as well as to the building of further almshouses. This points to yet further scope for future development of the charity's work.

Beyond this it would be premature to conjecture. What can be safely stated is that a minor social revolution is about to take place in the organisation of community care which will have a major impact on all those involved in caring for the elderly. It will offer new challenges to which St John's is well placed to respond, just as it has done for so many centuries.

Appendix: Heraldry in the Windows of the Chapel

Researched by Elystan G. Phillips (M.A. Oxon.).

East Window
a) North side: Vert a saltire engrailed Or between four crosses crosslet fitchy Argent (Devenish). (This is the only correct illustration of Devenish in a window.)
b) Apex: Or a saltire engrailed between four crosses crosslet Argent. (This is heraldically incorrect as it displays a metal on a metal field.)
c) South side: Gules three Paschel Lambs passant Argent, their banners each charged with a cross Gules (Lamb). (Paschal lambs should have haloes and lambs should have tails, but this must be a secular lamb.)

Windows
Or a saltire engrailed between four crosses crosslet fitchy argent (Devenish) impaling Quarterly Sable and Argent (Hoo).

South Side
a) Quarterly 1st and 4th Grand Quarters as Hoo. 2nd and 3rd Azure a fess between six crosses crosslet Or (St Omer) impaling Ermine on a chief indented Azure three ducal coronets Or (Lytton).
b) Azure an episcopal staff in pale Gold ensigned with a cross paty Argent surmounted by a pall of the last charged with four crosses formy fitchy Sable edged and fringed Gold (Abp. of Canterbury) impaling Quarterly Ermine and Gules in the 2nd and 3rd a goat's head erased argent (Morton). (Some blazons give only one goat and attired Gold. Cardinal Morton was Archbishop of Canterbury 1486-1500.)
c) As apex of east window impaling Quarterly 1st and 4th Argent a cross moline Sable (Copley); 2nd and 3rd Azure a fret Or (Etchingham).

The Ante-chapel
Devenish but this time the field has been changed to Azure and the saltire engrailed is Argent. Crest: a demi-tiger saliant Vert, holding a cross-crosslet fitchy Argent in his dexter paw.

Bibliography

Printed Sources

Atkinson, *Winchester Street Architecture*

Bird, (ed.), *The Black Book of Winchester*

Carpenter Turner, B. D. M., *Royal Hampshire County Hospital* (1990)

Carpenter Turner, B. D. M., *Winchester Hampshire Hogs: Vol II* (1991)

Cassan, *Lives of the Bishops of Winchester*

Deverell, J., *St John's Hospital and other Charities in Winchester* (1879)

Farley, J. S., (ed.), *The Usages of Winchester*

Farmer, D. H., *The Oxford Dictionary of Saints* (1978)

Gibson, J. S. W., *Monumental Inscriptions in Sixty Hampshire Churches*

Malmesbury, William of, *Gesta Pontificum*

May, (ed.), *The Somers Rentals*

Pevsner and Lloyd, *Buildings of England: Hampshire* (1962)

Stopher, *St John's Hospital, notes on its History in the last half Century* (1914)

Miscellaneous sources belonging to the city of Winchester

St John's Hospital Rolls, H.C.R.O. (a very large collection, not all in perfect condition)

Chamberlain Rolls, H.C.R.O.

INDEX